With much Love to John

In Search
Of My Father

The struggles of a family amidst adversity, and one woman's
dream while in search of her identity and meaning in life.

By

María G. Erazo-Luna and Adriana Kuhar M.

KAIROS TORA
Publishers

Kiaros Tora Publishers

Original title in Spanish, En Busca de Mi Padre, ©2012 by Maria G. Erazo-Luna and Adriana Kuhar M.

For more information about Kairos Tora Publishers visit:
www.KairosTora.com or
E-mail: Info@KairosTora.com
Bogota, D.C., Colombia

You may also order this book by visiting www.Amazon.com.
Due to the dynamic nature of the Internet, some web page addresses, or other connections in this book may have changed since its publication.

Translator: Adriana Kuhar
Editor: Jack Minor
Cover design: SaVon Clark
Stock Photography: Thinkstock
Portions of the Bible were extracted from the New International version.

ISBN: 978-0-9859763-0-9 (sc)
ISBN: 978-0-9859763-1-6 (hbk)
ISBN: 978-0-9859763-2-3 (e)
Revised: 9/2012

Dedication

I dedicate this book first to **my mother, Audelia Corona**, a valuable, courageous woman, whole-heartedly devoted in body and soul to rescuing her children from the claws of death through hunger, cold and violence. Her sacrificial love and life example merit her being made known. Although she realized she was alone with many children, without income and with little education, she attained her goal of providing a better future for my brothers, sisters and me where we were able to live with dignity. Her faith, anchored in God, planted within me the knowledge of our Creator's plan and purpose for each life. I hold dear and near to me her words of encouragement and admiration for me, even after having failed her so many times. She is the heroine of this story and the one who has motivated me to write.

To **my father, Reynaldo A. Luna**, who during the short time I knew him, left me valuable memories and lessons that guide my life to this day.

To **our aunt María Luisa Patino**, whom we endearingly nicknamed Lico, who helped us in spite of her countless limitations by introducing us to key contacts and teaching us, without complaining or focusing on her own obstacles. Without a doubt, Lico was an invaluable source of inspiration for us all. Aunt Lico, you are a brave woman of decision, and of a noble heart.

Also, **to each person who is struggling with difficult situations and thinks there is no way out** or any possible solution to their case. To you dear reader, I also dedicate this book. I trust that our story will assure you that anchored to the love of God and your family, nothing will be impossible.

Onward, and may your spirit be lifted high!

Contents

Acknowledgments

First, **I want to thank God**, our Creator and Protector, for guiding and shielding us even when we did not perceive His presence. I would also like to express my gratitude to the following people.

To **my husband Giovanni,** I will forever be indebted for his support and trust. His words of encouragement have inspired me to be a better wife, mother, daughter and friend. Not onlyzis he an excellent father to our three boys, but he has also motivated me to develop two of my passions, reading and writing. He has been patient even when my dream has required me to work during long night hours. No doubt, behind every great man there is a great woman; likewise, behind every woman that succeeds in the accomplishment of her goals, there is a great man that has provided his unconditional support. That man, for me, is you. I love you.

To **my children Milton, Dylan and Kayler**, you fill my heart and motivate me to be a better woman and mother. I long to leave you a valuable legacy with which to face the world when you are adults. May this legacy provide you not only with wisdom, but also prevent you from experiencing the difficulties and suffering that I experienced. Then my struggles will have not been in vain. I love you with all my heart and I know you will make valuable contributions to this world.

To **my pastors David and Gerry Christian**, your prayers and wise counsel have been priceless. May God continue blessing others through your lives.

To **Elias Yepez**; a talented and dedicated man of God who invested time analyzing this manuscript. His corrections and ideas were a great contribution. You can feel proud of your participation as an instrument in this final product. Remember, every seed you planted will give fruit. Thank you for being a great friend and one in whom we can trust.

To **Dante Villareal**, a mentor who challenged me to publish my experience, as well as carry out projects I felt incapable of achieving. Your knowledge helped me grow and your words enabled me to take firm steps. You have helped me discover a little more of my potential.

To **each of my brothers and sisters, Dioselina, Gabriel, Israel, Elia, Elena and Alma** I appreciate the contributions that directly or indirectly you have made to this project. Your trust and acceptance, in spite of the distance between us and above all, the unconditional love that we have for each other provide tremendous strength for me. You have inspired me and I trust that my example will also give you the strength to continue on the path before you. I love you profoundly.

To **Adriana Kuhar**, for having accepted the challenge of rewriting my manuscript, even when we had only met via the telephone. From that first phone call, and throughout our countless phone conversations, I cannot think of anyone more appropriate than you to take on this project and convert it into the final product we have in hand today. When Adriana first read the manuscript, she believed there was a lot a work ahead; however, recognizing it was a project that had the potential to impact many people, she accepted the challenge. I am convinced God provided the network of common friends to connect our paths. Although we have not yet personally met, as of the date of this final manuscript, Adriana is a great blessing for me. Her support in clarifying various stages of my life and her dexterity with the language have been valuable elements in writing this book that we share with you today.

Finally, **to every person God has brought to my life** to help me grow, come closer to Him, encourage and provide me with direction. Blanca Delgado who sustained my arms when my strength to finish this project was running out; Betty Ayala, Mayra Cortez, Maria Olga Mier, Mary Rodriguez, and Pastors Edgar and Erika Gomez, you are special to us. There are so many other people I could mention and while I do not do so here, I value what they have deposited into my life.

Preface

Maria stands out for her simple nature, cordiality and intelligence. Upon meeting her, one cannot help but to perceive her internal strength of character. She also possesses initiative, which has served her well in finding solutions to multiple and diverse obstacles. She is also a person dedicated to her family and to God.

Through enjoyable storytelling, Maria takes the reader from beginning to end using anecdotes of her life. Her life resembles the lives of many Spanish-speaking immigrants in the United States; however, what stands out the most is what she learned and the analysis that she incorporates into her life. Highlighted in her story is also the way she revives lost hope and reaches the dreams of her adolescence. This kind of human development, in the midst of conflict, motivates and challenges anyone who is facing difficulties.

If you arrived from a South American country or ever had the desire to immigrate to the United States, it is valuable for you to see this picture with greater realism. You will undoubtedly identify yourself with her struggles and triumphs. Her story will lead you to reflect on situations that mark the existence of a young girl, forging her character as she becomes a woman. However, though you may not be an immigrant you will feel interlocked with the force of her narrative and you will want, without a doubt, to know what will happen when you flip the page.

Primarily, what singles out Maria's story is that she has neither surrendered to multiple obstacles nor remained in the stage of mere regret. Instead, she drives us to think, question and clarify the matters that have meaning and value in life and embark on favorable change. I recommend, In Search of My Father, because I know that it will inspire you to count your blessings and extract the best from your failures.

Gilda Aguiar de Basave
USA Leader
Director of Educational Resources
Editor for John C. Maxwell
Bible teacher at Lakewood Church, Austin, Tx.

Introduction

Your daily decisions bring you closer or push you away from what you desire in life.

During moments of our development –childhood, adolescence, or adulthood– all people experience multiple disappointments, traumas and suffering, which lead us to think that our life makes no sense, and neither does the world around us. When facing such a hopeless perspective, if we look at the past, every person has legitimate reasons, as well as excuses for which he or she did not become who they would have liked to be. Can you identify with this feeling?

In addition, sometimes we feel ashamed of the mistakes we have made personally or of those made by our family members. Frequently, we also justify our lack of initiative and perpetual procrastination which in turn prevents us from undertaking goals that are significant to us. Excuses, shame, procrastination, mistakes and real negative life circumstances generate in us defeatist ideologies and evasive behaviors. We allow these feelings to invade us, and we end up blaming ourselves or others for the misfortunes we experience. However, the reality is that no one comes from perfect families, parents or situations and these are not reasons to deter us from our potential.

No doubt, this cumulus of negative reasoning is valid, although if we think about it carefully these kinds of thoughts only lead us to deeper disappointments. Worse yet, thoughts like these only distance us from assuming balanced personal responsibility. First, we are not responsible for everything that happens to us, or for other people's actions. Yet we are responsible for our own actions. Second, besides being responsible we are accountable for the use of the time, resources, and talent we have been granted during our life span.

Seeking to understand, instead of remaining in a state of inertia, may help you wake up to the truth that your life does have meaning. Though many years may have transpired and opportunities may have been wasted, your age is no excuse to continue clinging on to sorrow, and meditating on your stagnation. As long as your heart is beating, there is still a purpose for your existence here. Truly, you nor I need to remain in a state of failure, thinking about "what could have been and never was." You have the potential of assuming responsibility for you past, reorganizing your goals in the present, and undertaking alternatives for change towards your future. The person that understands this and assumes their responsibility will surely find paths that lead to victory over their obstacles and will outdo themselves beyond what they had imagined. Certainly, for those changes to be long-lasting, we need the power that comes only from our Creator and Sustainer.

Do you find yourself trapped in a reality of life that does not please you? Do you think about how you can turn your life around when you are facing so many adverse circumstances? On the one hand dear reader, do not expect that something will magically occur and everything will somehow change. On the other hand, do not go to the extreme of desperation believing you will never be able to pull out of the circumstances into which you were born or out of the place where you have arrived at due to your own decisions. Realistically, know that every change implies a process and every process implies time, effort, and persistence. If you are ready to put forth effort, invest time and persist, you can change your circumstances!

The secret to your change lies in acknowledging that your apparently small daily decisions either bring you closer, or push you away, from your desired outcome in life. You can sit and wait for a grand opportunity to come along; you can wait for that ideal person, or for the necessary elements to fly into your hands. In other words, you can remain static until you finally have all the conditions and time needed to make changes in your life. However, it is highly improbable that the elements you are waiting for will show up at once. Therefore, the wisest action to take is to start today, building little by little with what you have and doing it just from where you are. The reason for this is that every change you make, no matter how small, when performed day after day will receive the impact of cumulative effects and will indisputably modify your reality!

This text is designed to carry out individual and group work –with questions at the end of each chapter. The questions encompass critical personal and family occurrences that tend to make people come to a halt. The reflections will help you define your thoughts, feelings and everyday behaviors in a proactive manner. Remember that at the end of our earthly life, each person will be evaluated on their performance report for what they either did or failed to do with all of the resources and opportunities they received and how they utilized their time (life and experience), their talents (abilities and ideas), and their treasures (money, contacts, and influence). Thus the fact that our parents, teachers, friends, spiritual leaders, government or any other person or institution may have failed us is no excuse to learn how to make the best of our lives. So, don't "throw in the towel," or fall head first on the ground in defeat.

Pay attention and you will see that life is made up of a series of theoretical lessons, practical applications and their corresponding exams from which we are supposed to learn. These lessons not only spring forth from the mistakes we have made, but also from the falls and hard knocks we observe in other people's lives. God allows us to see these lessons along the way in order to mature and grow us as well as guide us to life alternatives that are wiser and healthier.

Consequently the problems that shake people up are not just situations that other people, systems or circumstances with power over us generate. Problems are also opportunities that the Author of Life allows so that we will come closer to Him. He is the only substance that has eternal value! Besides, if we are really paying attention, these negative circumstances can bring us to a better understanding of the purpose for our existence. Thus, problems also have a positive angle that can lead us to develop in many new dimensions. It depends on you how you chose to assume difficulties and conflict and what you extract from them.

When I received Maria's invitation to embark on the journey of writing this narrative and I got to know her story, it was evident that she had completely turned her life around from her initial destructive circumstances. Today she enjoys the many successes she longed for when she could see no way out of her problems. My desire is for these pages to serve as binoculars enabling you to see into the future. Also, for you to realize that your daily decisions are more powerful and important than you can imagine. Don't allow time to escape. Your time this day is valuable because not a single day that you waste will ever return. Time is a non-renewable resource, so take a little step today, make one single positive decision, and come closer to becoming the person you would like to be, like Maria did!

Two huge factors of inspiration are need and pain. I trust that Maria Erazo-Luna's account of her life may not just inspire you, but that it will also mobilize you to take actions that will change your current and future reality in many favorable ways.

Discover the deep value your life has, how you fit into other people's stories and the meaning that you have for your Creator. There are people that need you because heaven has entrusted in your hands tasks that only you can achieve. Have you discovered which tasks these are yet? If so, are you ready to carry them out? Remember, you are most fulfilled when you are becoming the person God wants you to be. No one else can fulfill the purpose for which only you are equipped.

Adriana Kuhar
Washington, D.C.
December 2011

THE BEGINNING OF MY STORY

The majority of people continue throughout their entire life in a quest, searching for genuine and unconditional love.

My Quest

As you may have discovered, the deepest longing of the human heart, including yours, is to be loved unconditionally. Although there are a large percentage of people who say they have found love, there are many others who deny they even need it. However, the majority of people continue seeking genuine and unconditional love, searching multiple forums and places during their entire lives, but in many cases never find it.

I believe that people have not found it because those who find unconditional love, without a doubt, begin to demonstrate it more and more by the very way they live their lives. Though they may be imperfect, their thoughts, feelings, words and actions reflect a different way of living. As they learn there is a better way of living, they start to develop a unique character, more in tune with the well-being of others. In other words, they learn that they do not have to be in conflict with themselves, with those around them, nor with their Creator. The love these people have found is not a human type of love, ephemeral and incomplete; it is the sublime, unmistakable, and unparalleled love of God.

When a person encounters this genuine, unconditional love, and begins to fill their soul with it, they spark a process of growing awareness that takes into consideration those whom they are surrounded by. They progressively reduce destructive behaviors towards themselves and others. As this process grows, the person learns to accept and love themselves as well as others, including those who harm them. It is a process beyond the innate structure of a human being and is only possible with divine intervention and transformation.

The fact that there is such a degree of cruelty and indifference in all types of societies –developed and affluent, as well as impoverished and illiterate, and among peoples of all races, tongues, and historical times– is an indicator that in six thousand years of human history, the majority of people still have not connected with that real love.

Today, if one asks a youth about love, they tend to respond according to what they have seen –strongly influenced by Hollywood's portrayal of love– a concept that reduces love to a frenzy of the senses, and the rubbing of erotic body parts or as Gandhi believed, "pleasure disconnected from conscience."

This counterfeit, cheap, and myopic notion of love without principles leaves those who practice it empty and unsatisfied. The love that deeply fulfills is the kind that is lived with commitment, truth, selfless giving, loyalty, confidence, generosity, integrity, justice and similar values that give meaning, depth and permanence to a loving relationship.

Moreover, a person who is learning to live by the principles of true love, divine love, continues growing in the capacity to love themselves first in order to then be able to love others. Genuine love leads one to experiment with self-acceptance, forgiveness and transparency… without which it is impossible to love one 's self or love others.

This is my story; the story of how, and where I sough this unconditional love, the various paths I took, and the various turns I made until I finally understood and assimilated the fact that I am loved, truly, completely and unconditionally not by a human being, but by the being that created me. Mine was a long and painful pilgrimage that I want to share, with the intent of possibly contributing significant elements to your own journey and quest.

Like you perhaps, I sought love in people, possessions, positions, pleasures and knowledge. Initially, I sought love in the people who gave me life. I expected my parents would fill all of my emptiness and wants and due to the fact that paternal love, in my case was intermittent –and suddenly became altogether inexistent– I came to long for it more intensely.

I also sought this love and acceptance in people who did not know the unconditional love of God, and could therefore not offer it to me. I did not understand that these people could not give me the love I longed for, not because they did not want to, but because they did not have it. I could not offer it either, nor could the things I purchased or experienced. With the passing of time, pleasurable sensations also dropped to an inferior level, since even these could not transmit the love I was seeking.

In addition, I focused on knowledge and learning. Though it is true that knowledge brings satisfaction, deep down it only fills a portion of the internal void that every person has. Because of its very nature, no created thing can permanently fill the need to be loved unconditionally.

Next, I will share with you the story of my family background and personal search.

Family Background

Far from civilization, in a remote location known as Michoacan, Mexico, there lived a few modest families. They shared their scarce economic resources and traditions among a small mountainous population, to which access was available only by foot or on horseback. There were no public utilities and their simple houses were made of brick with mud roofs and wooden siding.

Most of the ten families were connected by bloodline relationships and consisted of a father, a mother and between eight to twelve children. They were deeply rooted in tradition due to generations of living in isolation.

With time and before the coming of the television set in this region, the number of its inhabitants naturally grew. They had been able to build their own chapel, where they carried out religious services once a month with the rituals of the Catholic faith. This town also had a little school with three classrooms where teaching was imparted to children from preschool age up to sixth grade. During the school year, dedicated teachers would travel to towns located far away where they were well received in their student's homes. These teachers quickly became part of the family, because parents truly valued their labor.

However, after a child finished the sixth grade, there were no other options to continue studying beyond that. Instead, they had to travel to the nearest town, which was ten hours away. To get there they had to walk more than half the distance by foot, since there were no roads for vehicles to use. Because of this, the majority of people considered their education finished when they graduated from sixth grade, after which they dedicated themselves to agriculture or to hunting, as these were the only means for survival.

There, amidst the fruit trees, flowers, fresh water, laughter and dance, my parents, Audelia Corona and Reynaldo A. Luna, were born. Audelia, the eldest of 12 siblings, had to assume the role of their mother from a very early age, which forced her to abandon her education. Because she was the eldest, she had to stay home and help my grandmother with household tasks, while her younger brothers and sisters attended school. This was the inheritance –and what an inheritance, right?– of the eldest girls in our village.

Mother was a happy, creative and intelligent child in this civilization which was hidden from vehicles, noise, trash, and contamination that usually adorn large cities. She had dreams of achieving big things when she was older. One of her desires was to become a schoolteacher so that she could instruct those children, who like herself, could not leave the village for lack of greater income and training. Mother also felt happy serving the needy. However, her mother, my grandmother, was a domineering type of woman –to say the least– and somewhat of a bitter person.

Whenever mother would share her dreams with her, she would demolish them, bursting her bubble and saying they were nonsense. With someone like that, who would dare to dream, right? Despite all of this discouragement, she fantasized about achieving at least one of her desires. Her father was a calm, good-natured and loving man, who defended her from the constant insults and physical abuses of his humiliating wife, who had also grown up a victim of the same kind of treatment, perpetrated by her parents. In this manner, the denigrating and humiliating tradition was passed on from generation to generation.

In spite of grandma's offenses and abuse, mother did not give up on insisting she be allowed to attend school. Her persistence eventually paid off and at age 13 for the first time in her life, she was able to attend school during one year. Later on, when she was 17, she was able to attend school for another three years. This was all the academic preparation mother was able to attain through much sacrifice and dedication.

Likewise, my father came from a large and underprivileged family that lived in another town close to mother's. However, he was able to finish the 6 years of primary education offered there. Unlike mother, father studied under the compulsory mandate of his parents.

When mother was 20 and father was18 years old, they met at a dance in a family gathering. In those days this was the typical way people socialized and had fun, especially the youth of our towns. Shortly after meeting they began going steady, but mother was terrified of the reaction from her domineering mother if she ever found out. Finally, the inevitable occurred and grandma was infuriated with their relationship, strongly expressing disagreement as flames erupted from her mouth.

Nonetheless, the two of them continued seeing each other secretly and after two years of getting to know each, during the towns' celebrations they decided they wanted to marry. But the clever and ill-behaved grandma had another plan. She had already determined the fate of my poor Cinderella mother, committing her to marry another young man who she considered more responsible and from a more reputable family than father; despite mother not feeling the least bit attracted to him. To this day, my mother cannot explain how she succeeded in working up sufficient courage to refuse her mother's plans, but she did it and generated a bomb-like angry tirade on behalf of grandma. In view of these totalitarian and slavish reactions with the intent of depriving my mother of her liberty, as well as the physical violence that grandma exerted against her first born, my paternal grandparents accompanied my father to request mother's hand in marriage. Although grandmother was terribly upset, she had no remedy other than to accept because there were so many people opposing her plan. Then, for the last time she discharged her anger –a byproduct of her own frustration and bitterness– by beating mother up, as usual. Of course, it was not convenient for grandma that my mother marry since she was the one that helped with all the household chores and provided care for the younger children.

During these times, and in this place, there were no protection laws, nor support for victims of abuse. In fact, a beating on behalf of a parent was not even considered an act of violence with negative consequences for a person, when they were a minor. That society simply viewed it as a form of educating a child. Thus, up to that time, no one had been able to defend my mother from the domestic violence she suffered on behalf of her own mother, who was not even the evil stepmother in the story. On this occasion, not even her future husband could do anything about it.

It is therefore not difficult to imagine that when father asked mother to marry him, mother did not hesitate for a moment in accepting, not only because she loved him but also because she finally envisioned an end to her torture and could forever distance herself from the cruelty, abuse and domination under which she lived.

The story, from my father's perspective, was different. Father was my grandparents' favorite son; he was a dreamer, hard-working and a joyful person. He loved partying and within his means, he was always well dressed.

When my parents were married, the religious ceremony was quite simple. By then, grandmother had calmed down and resigned herself to the fact that the daughter who was her right hand would begin her own family; so both families attended the wedding. Mother wore a long white gown. It was a magical day for both of them, but especially for my poor mother whose dream was not only to come to the altar, but beyond the ceremony and the dress what she desired most was to build a home with her husband that would last a lifetime. She longed for the harmony and love she had not had in her own home growing up to reign there. Everything pointed to a united marriage, as it usually does at the beginning of every love story, in which both of them would attain their dreams; and so it was for a short while.

After the wedding, they went to live alone in a house that my paternal grandfather sold my father, for his wedding day. It was a small house made of adobe, where one could breathe fresh air and where they cohabited with little animals of all sorts. It had one bedroom, a kitchen and a patio surrounded by many fruit trees. There was not an abundance of riches, but they could eat healthy unfrozen food, non genetically modified, without preservatives, or colorants. Like the rest of the local population, my parents too would dedicate themselves to cultivating the land and hunting, as well as tending to their grazing animals, which they would not vaccinate or fill with hormones. Everything there grew wild just like in a little paradise.

The house was located one hour away from where my maternal grandparents lived –sufficiently far away from grandma's shadow so as to live peacefully. However, it was further out from the towns that sold medicines and other basic products for subsistence. Life there was not easy and for simple medical assistance, they had to walk several hours to the nearest town. Despite these circumstances, they were not subject to the stresses of modern life or enslaved to time. They did not steal hours from their rest or sleeping time and did not sacrifice personal relationships in order to obtain material goods. They had no foreman, or orders to produce more or perform more rapidly. They were not overcrowded in a dingy room or have to pay for their water or other services. They lived quietly and sweetly at a pace that promoted longevity –as a naturist would say. Although this beginning seems romantic, my parents were also planting the seeds of conflict and oppression.

I was born in that little house; the firstborn of this new home. During labor, mother fainted and those who were present thought she would die, because she was out for quite a while; however, God still had many plans for our lives. She had the support of a midwife who assisted the town families during childbirth, and was the most experienced person in the area. When tragedies happen, and there is no one to run to, people instinctively search for a miracle, whether they believe in God, and follow Him, or not. God is somewhat like a firefighter that we seek whenever we have an emergency; but once we overcome the difficult moment, we forget Him again. During that crisis, my grandmothers and other family members prayed to God requesting a miracle, and after several hours, mother began to recuperate.

My birth changed my parents profoundly, as I was the first fruit of their love. My father fell in love with me the minute he saw me. He protected me, not allowing anything bad to befall me and said that I would be a very intelligent girl because days after I was born I recognized his voice. From the beginning, he was a loving father, and I grew surrounded by the love of both mother and father. We lived in our first house until I was five years old. My siblings Dioselina and Gabriel, the first boy of the family were also born there. Up to that moment, unaware of the challenges that our parents were starting to have in their relationship, our childhood life was beautiful. Though we had few financial resources, we were happy just being together.

The Happiness of a Child

What young children desire most is to receive the love and attention of their parents. They yearn for the afternoon to come so their parents can return home from work and play with them. They love vacations with the whole family, laughter, new things and no matter how brief it is, a shared activity with mother, father, siblings and extended family. Each of these becomes a great project for a child. When parents participate in these activities, children not only learn, but they also enjoy the interaction more and it also generates memories that will forever be engraved in the hard drive of their computer: the brain.

Today, I remember that when I was young I felt happy with simple things. I found ways to have fun without having toys that large companies and stores advertise. I made dolls out of dried corn cobs and their clothes from the left over scraps of cloth that mother had used for making our garments. My siblings and I were creative and invented new games that would keep us busy for hours. This was far removed from today's society where children cannot live without their computers or their video games that suck them away from reality and family relationships.

Since our parents did not have the financial resources to buy us real toys, our greatest ally was our imagination –which this modern generation seems to lack. It is only with great difficulty that children and teens are able to create a game, outside of those advertised or focused on electronics. We didn't care about those things because we were happy playing with rocks, sticks, leaves, dirt and sharing our time together and with our parents. During those days when my father was busy cultivating the fields, my mother took care of us and cooked in order to take dad his meals. Occasionally, I would help mom with what I could, and performed some of the chores.

At the age of six, I started school. I would walk for an hour to the village where my maternal grandparents lived. Of course, grandmother had softened up by then, due to life's hard knocks. Several children of my village and I walked together as we played along the way on the unpaved road of which I enjoyed every step of the way. I shared some of these childhood adventures with my uncles and cousins who were also of school age. We would cut flowers, tell jokes and talk about stories and experiences. We would also create competitive games, all of which made the walk seem shorter. Once in a while, we encountered dangerous animals, but we always found a way to defend ourselves.

On one occasion, we were running alongside a small river when all of a sudden I heard a lot of noise in the bush, near the dirt road. The other children that were with us started screaming, warning me not to move. I did not understand why they were saying this, but when I stopped for a moment I realized I was surrounded by snakes that were crossing the road. Fortunately, these vipers were not poisonous and fled from humans, but for me this information was of little comfort as I was in a state of panic. After seconds, that seemed like an eternity, once they made their way across we were able to continue on our way to school. This experience gave me a phobia towards all types of insects and reptiles that I still suffer from to this day.

From that first year on, I loved attending school. Teachers, observing my desire to learn, encouraged mother to not let me miss classes. Besides the reptiles, at that age I did not know what fear or rejection were, nor had I encountered solitude, and abandonment. I just enjoyed each day with few material things, but with the necessary elements to live happily and satisfied.

Reflection

1. *What were the circumstances that motivated my mother's wedding? Of course, there was love, but she was also seeking an escape route from the servile life she was leading. Do you think those reasons were the best to start her own home? Why or why not?*

2. *What circumstances motivated your mother –or the person that raised you– to get married or leave home with their partner? Beyond love, what motivated you to start a new life with a partner?*

3. *My mother had to stop studying. Without academic preparation, or a good skill set of some sort, her possibilities of accessing a better-compensated job were limited. The lack of education reduced her options, and drove her children to a life of poverty. As a woman, in what ways are you preparing yourself to confront any future situation?*

4. *We get married, or start a romantic relationship, oftentimes unprepared, without knowing what each individual wants toward the future. Sometimes, the union is more hormone driven; there is not enough genuine love, or commitment, on behalf of the individuals involved for a sustainable relationship. Many of us began this type of relationship with a lack of communication about expectations. Even worse, is that few couples reach previous vital agreements. The following is a list of critical topics to consider and for which we need to have clarity before jumping into bed. It is not an exhaustive list, but you could start the dialogue and continue developing it as you go.*

   a. *What does your partner and what do you think about having children? (When, how many, how often...)*

   b. *How do you plan to share all of the household chores, and other responsibilities?*

c.   *How are you going to limit the influence of the mothers and fathers-in-law, siblings from both sides, and extended family? (Perhaps this is more prevalent in certain cultures).*

d.   *How do you plan to manage your finances? Will you save? Will you be compulsive buyers, or will you only purchase the things you really need?*

e.   *How do you plan to manage your relationship with God as a couple, and in the rearing of your children as you model their values?*

f.   *Do you think it is important for a couple to talk about these matters and reach agreements? This is something that needs to be done before committing to the closest relationship between two people, that can impact one's entire life. This relationship has the potential to provide or diminish psychological, physical and spiritual stability! It is better to make an effort to resolve differences early on, or end the relationship, when there is not an agreement on significant issues. Falling in-love with an illusion, to later suffer the consequences of blind love, is really not worth it! As a matter of fact, it is not conducive to happiness for either of the two parties involved.*

2

MY FATHER'S DECISION

He did not know how he broke my heart every time he left.

When I was six years old, my father decided to immigrate to the United States. He convinced mother it was the only way to provide a better financial situation for our family and to ensure we would not miss out on the opportunity to receive an education. Mother, desiring a better future for her children, supported him because she did not want to abandon her dream of having her children obtain an education. My parents lived during a time when there was a large exodus of people from rural areas of Mexico to larger cities both within and outside of the country. These people, hoping to improve their economic situation, sought to save money with two objectives in mind. First, to send funds back home in order to support their families, and secondly, to save up enough money to purchase property, build a house, and set up a home business, just as many people still hope to do today.

For people of little means, leaving their country was the only viable option if they wanted to leave a family heritage. Risk takers, while considering the many dangers to which they were exposed still opted to leave; whereas others attempted to improve their family's financial condition through traditional methods such as agriculture. Nevertheless, not everybody had the opportunity to own land and harvest it to sell crops and improve their lives. Some of those with land provided work opportunities and hired nearby workers to pick crops.

In our case, my father's land only produced enough food for our family. If father wanted to earn more money, he could only aspire to work as one of the hired hands on grandfather's land, or on the land of other relatives who grew corn. Because father came from a large family and was one of the younger siblings, the probability was that once the family property was divided between them, his inheritance would be very small.

After starting his own family, and facing the reality of providing for his children, father wanted to do something different so that we could have a better life than he had had, which would include a greater opportunity for education and health. His search for a brighter future drove him to make the decision that many others have made, which would ultimately change the course of our lives.

At my young age, I did not realize what was happening; I had not experienced the financial and social pressures that force adults to make harsh decisions, motivated by love. Every night, my parents would do their usual round to check on each of us and ensure we had blankets because the nights were cold and the frigid air pierced every orifice of our humble house. Father did not usually sit beside us before bedtime, but on a certain occasion he did, as he spoke with mother and fondled my hair saying, "Look at our daughter. She is beautiful! She is pretty and intelligent and every day she surprises me even more. I am very proud of her and I know she will achieve important things in her life."

He promised mother that he would do whatever was in his power to help me accomplish my goals. Then he kissed my forehead, covered me, and as he used to say to me lovingly, "Good night, golden beak."

I will never forget that night, though he soon forgot his promise. I am conscious that the profound love our father had for us was in part, the motor that propelled him to think of other options in life. From his point of view, the best alternative was for him to leave us and go to work far away, even though this would entail his separating from us. Today I understand that at the time my parents made that decision they did so believing it was the best they could do for us. However, I have learned that there are other ways to respond when facing financial challenges. Though I don't judge them for their decisions, I would have preferred it if they would have opted for a solution that would not have separated our family.

What is sacrifice?

In essence, a sacrifice is giving up or surrendering something that is valuable for a person for for the sake of something that they perceive as having a higher value. Motivated by that profound love, most parents tend to be people who are willing to sacrifice their own comfort and interests for the well-being of their families. Although parents may make decisions thinking they are best for their children, they may not have weighed many of the future consequences of their actions.

How many decisions do we make for conveniences sake or for the well-being they seem to provide in the short term, rather than for their long-term value? In general, we perceive that more money or a better house and more things are of more importance than being together, demonstrating our dedication with actions, or transmitting values that endure in the heart and conscience of our children for a lifetime. Childhood is a treasure that passes all too quickly and never comes back. One can remake material fortunes, but time lost will never again return.

When the day of my father's departure to the United States came, I did not even really remember how we said goodbye. I think he did it at night so that we would not see him leave. He knew it would affect us deeply, especially me, because I was the eldest and was quite attached to him. I would have tried to prevent him from leaving because I was used to spending lots of time working in the fields with him and delivering the food mother prepared. The day he left, I just remember waking up and not seeing him. When I asked mother, she said he had gone to work far away, but that he would soon be back.

From then on, nothing was the same. I felt the tremendous void that his absence created in me. I was afraid at night and felt different when I was among the other children who were living with both parents. For the first time, I felt mistrust for the people around me, while a deep loneliness engulfed mother, my siblings and I. Although my grandparents would visit us, the security that father's presence imparted on us was evident.

Grandma and grandpa assisted mother with chores and the tasks in the field, while helping take care of us; however, I began to see the world in shades of gray. My father's absence made the colors that had illuminated my days become dark.

Our lives had not noticeably changed outwardly, but the pain that I felt due to father's departure drove me to isolattion. As soon as I was out of the classroom, I would lose all notion of time. In my heart, I yearned for and awaited father's return on the same road he had left. Nevertheless, days passed by slowly, and what I longed for most did not occur. For an entire year, he did not return home. It was too long a time to wait for a child who desired to be in her father's arms.

Although parents would perhaps perform a better job raising their children by teaching them values that transcend and impact their lives, in contemporary society they frequently dedicate time to multiple distractions –television, video games, a professional career, sports…– and they tend to neglect essential dialogue, and activities that are truly shared, not just those they observe together. With the passing of time, parents discover how much they have lost. In my case, to have grown up apart from my father marked me, leaving within profound imprints of abandonment and loneliness.

Disconnected from my father

During the time my father was working in the United States, communications between him and the rest of us were almost non-existent. The days where telephone service was only available in a town several hours away from our house is far removed from today's cellular age. We were able to call only every two to three months when he had saved money and was able to send it to mother. She would then go to town, pick up the funds and kill two birds with one stone by calling and speaking with him for a few minutes. Occasionally, he would write letters that we would pick up when we went for the money. Time elapsed and little by little the communication between us turned colder and colder, not just between my parents, but also between my father and the rest of his family. He lived outside of our world in the mountains, where days passed by amidst nature's calm ways in a contemplative sort of life.

Now, father was acquainted with other people and new customs amidst a busy life-style where the language and culture were still foreign to him. However, that life somehow swallowed him up and eventually became more important to him than we were. Those of us who lived in his past had become just a distant dream. Albeit, mother continued to faithfully wait for him, along with her children. In the afternoons, she used to make tea from fresh lemon leaves she would cut from the trees. We would sit in the back patio of the house while we observed splendorous sunsets that disappeared behind the mountains while mother would entertain us with her amazing narratives and surprising stories.

One dark evening, we were sitting and talking with mother and some of my aunts outside our grandparent's house and looking at the stars and moon.

Suddenly, we saw a light in the distance getting closer to the dirt road that came into town. My aunts started to joke, saying that it was possibly my father returning. As I listened to them, I felt as if my heart was pumping out of my chest, but I said nothing, because I did not believe it was possible. Anxiously, we waited for the light to come closer so we could see the details. As it got a little closer, my heart told me that it was him, but I had waited so many nights wishing to hug him that I did not want to suffer once again from a mere illusion. I had so resigned myself to his absence that my mind denied conceiving that possibility. I truly believed I had lost my father forever. In my childhood mind thoughts of the past were nebulous. Nevertheless, to my great surprise, *it was him* and he had returned home that night! Daddy had returned home from his trip, what a joyous night!

We spent hours and hours talking and looking at the presents he had brought us, while he held me in his arms. I remember he brought a small guitar with which he sang a few songs to me until I fell sound asleep. Initially, I did not want to sleep for fear that he would vaporize while I rested. I never again wanted to have to leave his side. My father was a very warm hearted and happy person with his children. I admired him and felt secure beside him. On this occasion, he stayed with us for a few months, only to plan his next trip. Compared to the time of his absence, the time he was home with us passed much too quickly for me.

Of course, without asking for my opinion, once again father left thinking that I did not understand. He did not know how he broke my heart every time he left, yet it became customary to see him come and go... come and go... Amidst this situation, mother gave us all the attention and love she could and our extended family made our time enjoyable.

We continued helping our uncles and grandparents with chores as we persisted with school tasks; however, it was my constant thought and desire that time would speed up to see father once again. Contrary to what all of us wanted, father continued working in the United States and over the next four years his letters began to come less frequently like our thoughts about him. His presence became a distant memory creating a gap that separated our family little by little each day. Finally, mother decided we would go to live with our maternal grandparents. We had to abandon the house we had grown up in forever. Nonetheless, grandma's house was large, with lots of land where they grew corn and fruit. The crops generated sufficient funds to purchase the goods needed for a large family, and the animals they hunted or fished were a complement to the family's nutrition.

Thus, our lifestyle did not change much. We had become accustomed to father's unending voyages; this was especially true for mother. Undoubtedly, the absence of a father often leaves voids that can last a lifetime. One of the reasons why my maternal grandmother had so adamantly protested the marriage of my parents was because father's family was known for emigrating to other parts of the country and abroad, leaving their wives and children behind with relatives who eventually had to look after them. Grandma was certainly right on that one!

My father was an extrovert and a dreamer. He liked to meet different people and constantly change environments. He was not a conformist and he had many goals. His personal challenges drew him away from a typical family man who is happy to have a little house and some land on which to grow provisions. By the looks of it, grandma had not been mistaken when she had warned mother, before her wedding, that father was an unstable man. Even so, mother had been happy with him up to that point and supported his decisions.

My grandparent's ranch was peaceful. It was located between a large river and a small stream. While grandpa and my uncles focused on the agriculture, mother and grandma took care of house chores, prepared food and provided for everyone of their children's needs. They had few preoccupations and dedicated time to us and provided us with love. I remember that several of my uncles, who also lived in the United States, would visit us and bring news, letters and money from father.

With the money that dad sent, mother would use a portion for our sustenance and the rest she would save with the goal of eventually purchasing a plot. The plan was that later on, father would return to farm his own land. Slowly, our financial situation was improving though the image of our father vanished almost entirely from the panorama.

Father was away during one year before he returned to Mexico from that trip. He had become accustomed to his other life and no longer liked the idea of living in the countryside. His thoughts had surely changed, and he had a new plan for our lives.

Reflection

1. *We pursue golden dreams, thinking that money is the most important element (although we may not express it, we live as if it were), even more important than the people we love. Remember, the time we do not spend with our loved ones, will never return. What have your parents sacrificed and how have their decisions affected you?*

2. *Based on your experience, what will you do differently in the relationship with your partner and your children?*

3. *Egocentric people, who exclusively think about their needs, and desires, tend to cause immesureable pain and destruction to those around them. Consider your goals, dreams, and aspirations and what you are willing to sacrifice in exchange for these. Is it worth it? Are you willing to sacrifice even your children? Why or why not?*

4. *If you consider that your work, education, travel, or any other goal is more important than a loved one, perhaps the best thing you can do is to live your life alone. That way, you will not hurt another being that loves you. (i.e. a spouse, partner, or a little one) because your lack of commitment, when you choose not to share your time, money, or effort, it is a true indication that you are not ready for a long-lasting relationship.*

3

PRIORITIES

During that time, father did not work because he was enslaved to the sad and destructive drinking habit.

Father's priorities had changed as he lived among other people with different cultures. He now had different ambitions and was willing to continue sacrificing his family relationships in order to obtain a lifestyle that, according to him, was better. However, not considering the consequences of his decisions he set new goals in order to scale up that social ladder and this time the change would be even more drastic for all of us.

As on previous occasions, he knew he would persuade mother onece again. After all, mother was subject to his will; she knew that her opinion would not be taken into consideration for the final decision. This new adventure consisted of moving us from the ranch to the city of Morelia, the capital of the Michoacan state, where my paternal grandparents had gone to live a few years earlier. From where we were currently living, Morelia was ten hours away by bus.

When father proposed the new plan to mother, she was not fully on board with it. The only environment she had known was her village and the nearby towns which she visited whenever we needed medical or dental care. Although this was the most significant change mother had faced, she knew that as long as father was beside her it would be a good opportunity to improve their relationship, which wasn't on the best of terms due to the bitter experiences of the past and the distance he had maintained by living abroad. Mother wanted to trust him and his decisions again, almost blindly. She suffered in silence while we, her children, ignored what was going on between them behind the closed doors of their bedroom.

Through the art of manipulation, using words and intimidation, father convinced her, saying we would have even better opportunities in the city. Father knew that to have a brighter future, we needed education beyond the sixth grade. Mother accepted because she also wanted something better for us. So, they sold the land and the house in the countryside, which they had purchased with such immense efforts and we left for the city. The plan was for us to live with our paternal grandparents while we found a house of our own.

At this time, my parent's relationship had experienced severe difficulties. One of the main issues was chauvinism. Father had the ability of manipulating and intimidating mother. He was used to deciding and having plans carried out his way.His ideas and actions excluded mother's opinions. In his parent's home it was the same way and he continued the pattern with mother.

Good byes

Living at the ranch, we had been used to running freely in the fields and swimming in the river during long hours. Our uncles had taught us to fish and hunt birds. If we felt like eating fruit, we only needed to go to the back yard and pull whatever was in season off the trees. For fun, during those long afternoons, we would make sand and stone castles on the riverbank. In the evenings, we lit campfires in the yard and toasted green fruit over the flames.

On weekends, my maternal grandfather, Francisco, would sit beside us to enjoy the fire's warmth while telling us intriguing tales of his youth. His words ignited our young imagination; anxious to know and explore his world of fictitious narratives of witches and magic –which according to him he had seen flying over trees– as well as other stories about his ancestors. Those evenings beside him were like sitting in front of a television set and watching the most intense movies. We did not have a radio either, but we had a grandfather who could change reality with his memories and imagination. At night no one wanted to be the first or the last to enter the house, as we anticipated that some of the characters that granddad had just described with a luxury of details could surprise us.

We truly enjoyed those times together and in spite of being sleepy, no one wanted to sleep. During nights with a full moon, we would swim in the river at dawn. In the evenings, one could only hear the songs of frogs and other animals. Life there was simple and time seemed to stretch in that beautiful place. The greatest dangers there were the scorpions and reptiles that slid in under the wooden doors or between the beams of the house, especially on rainy days where it seemed as if we were not the only ones seeking a dry corner somewhere.

Grandpa Francisco was a humble, hardworking, loving and noble man. I have never known another person like him. I never saw him hurt grandma or act disrespectfully towards others. He taught my uncles to work hard and did so with his own example; he was the first to wake up and drink some lemon leaf tea before he left to carry out his chores at dawn. Besides all this, he taught us love and reverence towards God.

Grandma Zenaida, would wake the older children up early so that we would help with the chores. We ground corn to make tortillas and prepared atole, a corn drink, so that when the sun rose the table was ready for grandpa and my uncles to have breakfast before they left to work the fields. After we finished our tasks, the girls would go to the river to wash the plates and bathe. My siblings and I would spend hours having fun on the river bank, since we knew that when we returned home we would again have to help prepare the food for lunch and of course, it was more enjoyable to play. It was fascinating to see how the sun slowly rose over the mountains, reflecting brilliant rays of light on the river waters. In certain places, we could see the bottom under the water with clarity. This was a tempting invitation to submerge ourselves and come up again to play and then jump from the rocks to the edge of the river.

My grandmother had a strong character —as you have already heard. We obeyed her immediately, as she was strict in her dealings with her children and grandchildren. However, she cooked delicious meals and she and mother taught us how to carry out many household tasks. She was dedicated and organized, including the household finances. Her children sought her out when they needed to make important decisions because they respected her advice.

Although mother feared sharing father's decision to take us to the city with grandma she finally did so, knowing grandma would be quite upset. Mother had never known what it was like to separate from her family and put so much distance between them. Grandma told her to think through her decision well since she would not be able to help us from afar. Mother was between a rock and a hard place while listening to grandma's counsel and father's proposals. However, as a married woman who felt she needed to continue walking beside my father in spite of the difficulties in their relationship, she decided to follow him in his new adventure.

During those years at our maternal grandparent's house, Francisco and Zenaida, my aunts, and uncles, Irma, Victorino and Alfredo —ages 14, 13 and 11, respectively– and Eva, my mother's youngest sister who was 10, my parent's and all of us children lived with them. Mother's older siblings already lived in the United States. When father arrived, ready to take us to the city they had not prepared us sufficiently for the change. They told us suddenly that we would be leaving to go to a new place far away and that we needed to organize our suitcase, which would have very little in it. As we said our good-byes to our grandparents and uncles, we all cried endlessly. My grandfather could not stand the idea of seeing us depart, so he hugged us and with tear-filled eyes left for work very early that morning. I saw his watery eyes and my heart broke because I loved him deeply. He had in fact replaced the father figure we had lacked during those last few years. The day we left our maternal grandparent's ranch generated deep sorrow in us all once again.

Full of nostalgia and conflicting emotions, we made our way towards the city to our new and better life. I remember we left carrying a few garmets and of course, many dreams. I was almost eleven years old and my youngest sister was one year old; we were a total of six siblings. Having sold our land and house in a short period, father was now transporting us on an old truck to our new destination. The truck was so old that during the trip the nauseating gasoline smell and the intense noise coming out of the engine made our journey very long. We felt sick and had strong headaches; however, we could only hear our parents excitedly talking about their plans once we arrived in the city. Nevertheless, my thoughts were heading in another direction. I was enveloped in the life we were leaving behind, and thought about my grandparents and uncles.

Between stops to eat and go to the bathroom we finaly arrived at my paternal grandparent's house in the evening. Mother and I along with my siblings felt strange; it was as if we had arrived in another country. Perhaps it had to do with the different environment; the auto noises, the many people everywhere and the houses that were so close together.

As days passed, we confirmed that everything was quite different. We could no longer run freely through the fields or remain alone outside, without an adult present, because of the multiple dangers of the city. As of that moment, our lives changed radically. We were happy to be near our paternal grandparents, especially grandma Carmen who was a loving and patient woman. However, we never forgot our maternal grandparents and uncles we had left behind.

Prolonged Absences

Months passed by and little by little father continued spending the money that mother had so sacrificially saved. During that time, father did not work because he had the sad and destructive habit of drinking. This vice had him on the streets with his friends nearly every night, misspending the little money we had left. No matter how much mother restrained from spending in order to avoid wasting funds that were intended to buy our house, father demanded that she give him the money. According to him, he had earned it and had the right to spend it –a typical chauvinist and arbitrary answer that does not contemplate the well-being of the family as being more important than personal and temporal pleasures.

Although mother had suceeded in the difficult task of saving these funds, by denying herself and her children even the most basic of needs, father was oblivious. Mother feared his domineering character, as much as or more than she feared her mother. She realized she had left one oppressive situation in the past and had fallen into another that was probably worse, because now she was an adult and had many children all or whom would bear the consequences.

Nonetheless, her upbringing had accustomed her to not go contrary to her husband's desires. Mother had learned to be a submissive woman, quiet and reserved. According to her traditions, in the majority of cases men had the last say and the role of women was that of submitting to their orders, no matter how absurd they seemed. Nonetheless, in her home growing up it had not been so. My maternal grandmother had run a matriarchal system where she exerted dominance and her power was demonstrated by having the last word. The truth of the matter for mother was that her opinion had no weight. Although she carried on as best she could once again she felt insecure, questioning what would happen to us once the money was gone. In silence, mother suffered. Frightened and bereaved, she devoted her energies to taking care of us the best she knew how and continued sending us to school.

Innumerable times during this period father would come home drunk at dawn. He was used to beating mother up and taking out his anger on her after his street fights and rivalries with friends. She now had less support than ever and no one could help her. With very little money, so many little children, and now living ten hours away from her family, she felt obliged to remain by father's side. Besides, she truly believed that the best she could do for her children was to stay with dad, even though he was a bad example for them.

My paternal grandparents, Guadalupe and Carmen, did not approve of father's actions; though unfortunately my grandfather did not exercise much authority over his adult son. Besides, they did not have a close relationship. My grandmother had advised and urged father to distance himself from his drinking friends and to focus on his family, but father did not listen to her either. He would get angry saying he was tired of her "antiquated sermons," as he called them. The months rolled by and when he realized that we no longer had enough money to purchase a house in the city, my father once again decided to travel to the U.S.

So, he prepared the details before his departure. First he rented a house, near our grandparents, since we were a large family and could no longer live with them. However, to everyone's surprise, mother told us she was five months pregnant and expecting her seventh child.

Father said his plan was to work at least one more year and return with sufficient funds with which to build both a house and establish a business in the city. Nevertheless, it seemed customary for dad to get mother pregnant and then leave when the most difficult part of dealing with a newborn came, which required support during sleepless nights and help with the older children.

In 1989, father once again said good-bye. He departed for the United States leaving us with mother in an unknown city, with the hope that as before, he would send money for our financial support. Mother only had enough time to take care of all of us while the eldest children continued attending school.

The first months passed with the same normalcy we were already used to. Finally, mother gave birth to Alma. Father called more frequently because iphone and mail services in the city were more readily available than in the country. He also continued sending us money... and another year went by.

I also sent father letters which included lists of things I wanted him to bring me. When we spoke by phone he told me to ask for all that I wanted because he would bring it to me. I lived in a world of illusions and though I missed father, I had the expectation he would return with many gifts and never leave us again.

After that year, at my young age I caught on that something strange was occurring. I saw that mother was sad and cried during much of the night. She constantly looked worried. Mother longed for father to return and help her raise their seven children. She told father on the phone that she did not care if they did not have enough money to open up a business. She needed him to help educate and take care of us. In addition to the problems between them, seven children were a huge responsibility for one person.

I was twelve then, yet mother did not tell me much of what was going on because she thought I was too young and would not understand. One day, grandma Carmen came looking for mother because daddy was calling her. It had been some time since he had last called and mother was joyous. In that conversation he told her he was very sad and lonely and wanted to come back to live with us. Mother encouraged him to do so immediately because we desperately needed him. Mother hoped and felt they could get by If they were together. He promised that he would return in a few weeks. This was their last conversation.

Reflection

It was sad, but necessary, to confront myself with my reality and that of many Latin-Americans who leave our countries in search of golden coins. Frequently, we allow the shining light from those coins to blind us with a life-style that developed countries offer. We exchange the emotional, psychological and spiritual well-being of our families not just for the supply of basic needs, which is understandable, but we re-organize our priorities based on material possessions.

1. *Too many immigrants risk their lives while playing with the well-being of those for whom we supposedly say we are fighting for. Our ideals of traveling abroad become stories of abandonment of our wives and children, whom we leave unprotected and affected for the rest of their lives. One cannot deny the benefits of living in a land that offers opportunity and even the possibility of sending money to the family when they need it. However, it would be wise to weigh the advantages and disadvantages for all those involved. It is time to question if it is worth the sacrifice in general, and the deterioration of family relationships, as if material things were the only and most important element to consider. If this is your case, are you conscious of what you are sacrificing?*

2. *Because I lived this situation first hand, it prompted me to reflect concerning the lack of material things that so many families experience. Governmental organizations, private, social, and religious organizations –including relatives with good intentions and a genuine desire to help– have made people with few financial resources dependent on the help they give. They think these are good works and ignore the fact that even to help, one heeds to know how to help, how much and when it is wise to extend that help. This must be done to prevent stimulating a beggar's mentality which can hurt a person's dignity and worsen an individual's, a familiy's or a group's condition.*

3. *We were created with the desire to live and fight for, as well as to conquer our dreams. If we easily obtain our dreams, this can kill the motivation which is the motor of our lives. Therefore, when possible, we dignify a person more by giving them work, teaching them a trade and listening to them rather than giving them food or basic necessities over and over again. It is one thing to offer temporary aid during an economic or health crisis or when there is a tragedy –natural disaster or conflict– but another very different thing to generate an indefinite and unhealthy dependence that kills a person's self-esteem and initiative. The old saying goes that it is better to teach a person to fish than to keep giving them the fish. How can you best help those in need?*

4

BEYOND DESPERATION

> *I heard her cry during hours until she would fall sound asleep from exhaustion.*

Days, weeks, and months passed by until they became a monotonous routine in which father did not return or even call. Although we sent letter after letter with the hope of his response, he never wrote back. The last letter I sent him said:

> *"Daddy, if the reason why you are not coming back soon is that you don't have sufficient money to buy me all that I have asked for, I want you to know that I don't want you to bring me anything. The only thing I want is to see you and for you to be with us. Please forgive me for being so self-centered and asking you for so many things. Mom, me, and my brothers and sisters miss you terribly! I love you very much!*
>
> *Your eldest daughter, Lupita."*

To this day, the words I wrote him are engraved on my soul because I wrote them with the faith of a child, trusting that daddy would read them and return home soon. However, that never happened. My parents did not argue during their phone calls therefore, there were no apparent reasons for their lack of communication. Father simply stopped calling and writing and stopped sending the funds that were vital for our survival: our only source of financial support. He had disconnected completely from everyone, including his parents and siblings. No one ever heard from him again, knew anything about his whereabouts or heard of anything happening to him.

Our growing sadness and hopes of seeing him again diminished. It seemed as if the earth had swallowed him up. We knew we could not look for him in a country so large and far away as was the United States from Morelia.

Although father had other siblings in the United States, they did not live with him. Neither they nor other relatives, friends or acquaintances could give us news about his whereabouts. His brothers and relatives looked for him in places where they knew he had worked and lived, yet no one could give us any information about him. Mother and grandma called the last telephone numbers they had for him; however, the answers were in English and they could not communicate. Frequently, they sought the intervention and favor of God. Yet even heaven remained silent.

I too tried to call. I learned a few words in English in case someone answered, and purchased calling cards with my savings. I would call, hoping daddy would answer me. I reasoned perhaps he was angry with mother and that could be the reason he did not answer. The people that did answer the phone either did not know father or simply did not understand us. I did this for several months with no results and without mentioning it to mother. Though we did everything in our power, we never heard from him again!

Several versions of his disappearance floated in the air and in the memory of his relatives. What we did know and were sure of, was that father had obtained his legal residence through amnesty granted by the government of the United States in 1985. Nonetheless, the government never sent us any communication concerning him either.

He disappeared without leaving a trace! He left incognito even to those who loved him. My grandma remained with the deepest longing for the return of her son and carried this pain in her soul to the tomb.

Hitting Rock Bottom

When father disappeared, the situation for mother and us worsened. She had never worked in the city. She did not even know how to use public transportation; except for the taxi when she went to pick up the funds that father sent or when she took us to the doctor and had to take the bus downtown.

Mother was a very dedicated woman who never left us alone. She did not go on trips or leave the house unless she had a reason; even then she did not go out alone. Once again, the money father had sent that she had saved, was diminishing. I was aware that each time she was buying less and less food.

However, as an excellent administrator mother miraculously stretched that money and was even able to use a portion of those funds to purchase a small one-bedroom house so she would not have to keep paying rent, which she would not be able to continue doing anyhow. These were hard times for my mother, who was alone in the big city with seven little ones. My maternal grandmother was the only one who visited us frequently and helped with what little funds she could.

All of us children slept together on one bed while mother slept on the floor. I remember when it rained a lot; the water would come in through the broken roof tiles. The nights were cold and I would wake up at dawn with a bone-penetrating chill. I would hear mother cry in silence, not wanting to wake us. I heard her crying for hours until she would fall asleep from exhaustion. With all my heart I wanted to console her, yet I did not know how to do it.

As the eldest sibling and conscious of the situation, I felt desperate with this reality. We lived in a state of permanent uncertainty, not knowing if we would have enough food for the next day. I could not concentrate in school, being absorbed in thoughts about mother since she remained at home with my younger brothers and sisters, often times without food to nourish them.

I felt impotent at twelve years of age, understanding the probability that father would never return and without having a realistic way to wake up from that daily nightmare. We had hit rock bottom and we could fall no deeper!

Under pressure, I began to think of options to help mother bring more money home. I proposed several alternatives, among them were that I could look for work after school or that she could work during the day; we also thought of asking father's family to help with my younger siblings so that mother could go out and sell tortillas on the street. Due to the dangers in the city, mother did not agree with me working since I was still young. Above all, she did not want me to be alone.

On a certain evening, I heard her cry nonstop for hours which deeply saddened me. Finally, I came close to her. Though the pain was deep, at the same time I thought we needed to discuss some of the options that I was proposing to find work. I sat in front of her in the dark and said, "Mother, I understand how sad you are because father has not returned; but it's time you do something about it! Otherwise, all of us are going to die of hunger and cold."

I told her she needed to get up the next day and look for work wherever she could to earn some money. In addition, I asked, "What are you going to do now? … You must be thinking of something, because time is passing by, and by merely crying you will not resolve anything!"

Perhaps, I did not understand everything I was saying that night. God used me to shake mother up with that message, although at the moment I thought it was desperation that drove me to react that way. She remembers that since that moment, she woke up. My words shook her to the core and brought her to decide she should do something or else tragedy would befall us and she would be to blame. That night, I suggested she go to the local food market to look for work since it was near our house. She was used to buying food there and several local restaurants were available where she could work making tortillas or preparing meals. Another alternative was to find work cleaning houses. Crying, mother responded, "Honey, I have thought about these options, yet the reason I hold back is your little siblings. What can I do with so many little ones while I go to work? Who will take care of you and prepare the meals? Besides, I don't know how to use the transportation system, nor do I know the city well. Where do I start? I feel as if the world has fallen on me, and I don't know what to do."

I told mother that I could help when I got back from school and we could request grandma's help in caring for my younger siblings during the day. We also had an aunt whom we had endearingly nicknamed Lico, who visited us on occasion. Her life was quite complicated. She had five kids and was a single parent. Her husband had been in jail for several years and his sentence demanded many more. Lico's children were about our age. Worse yet, she had suffered from paralysis that had immobilized half of her body, from her face to her feet. She walked with difficulty and could do some work but only with one hand.

Lico was my example to motivate mother. I reminded her of how, in spite of her many limitations, she strove to support her children. In Mexico, as in many other nations on the path to development, there are few programs available to aid impoverished families. Mothers with small children receive some aid from relatives when they can or resort to public charity. For the most part, poverty is exacerbated hundreds of times over for those who have physical ailments or impediments.

This cruel reality is even more of a disgrace among government officials, in impoverished nations, who do not strive to protect the least favored because they are more interested in accumulating wealth for themselves, than aiding the people who literally cannot aid themselves wither because they are too small, too old or because their body has betrayed them.

This was our reality. We were completely marginalized and no one cared to help us. Even the teachers at school knew our plight and that my father did not live with us. Nevertheless, it never occurred to them to ask us if we needed anything. I don't mean to judge and most likely they only had enough for their own families, but we all have the capacity to influence others and take collective action. If we don't have personal financial resources, we can mobilize others who have more than enough or can help by providing if only temporarily work. It is in essence more an issue of one's desire, a wish to help those in need rather than observe the scenario from the other side of the fence, with indifference.

Often we did not eat during the day because we had nothing to take to school. We could only sit and watch the other children enjoy their meals while our mouths melted with desire and our intestines loudly craved miniscule rations of food still in our bellies over which parasites were fighting. There were no school lunch programs either, where we could benefit from a breakfast, nor did we have friends we could go to for help.

On top of that, we were the laughing stock of all those who lived with both parents. Most classmates knew us by the nickname, "the orphans." They constantly mocked us over our old clothing and school uniforms which were passed down because we had no money to purchase new ones every year. The worst of it all, as I saw it, was that I could not talk with daddy at the end of the day when I got home to tell him about the cruelty of which we were victims, so that he could encourage or defend us. Mother was timid, so she never communicated with our teachers regarding the intense mocking or requested their help regarding our situation. In those dire circumstances, it was easy to lose hope, to despair and believe that our situation would never change!

On a certain occasion, aunt Lico came to visit us with her five children. Bearing my plan in mind, I asked her about the possibility of going with her to the places she went so we could also work. Due to her fears and preconceptions, mama did not agree because my aunt not only received help from wealthy people but also begged on the streets. She used to send her three eldest to school while she walked throughout the city with the youngest, begging for money.

Sometimes, she found people with sensitive hearts that felt compassion when observing her physical condition. They would give her clothing, food and shoes for her and her children. Some families even invited her to come back weekly so they could continue helping. Perhaps these people reasoned that it could have been them in Lico's shoes and surely they would have hoped that others had a drop of compassion, a grain of energy and decisiveness and a cup of love to help. Aunt Lico was a resolute and courageous woman with tremendous internal fortitude. In spite of her impediments, she nourished and dressed her children arming herself with great audacity in order to achieve her goal. I will never forget this. She inspired me and gave us the certainty and impulse necessary to believe that likewise, we could pull out of that horrible situation in which we felt we were drowning. We greatly admired and respected aunt Lico, and mother was aware that her enthusiasm and persistence were the only tools that Lico had to survive during such a long time with her children.

In spite of our poverty and calamity, mother's conditions were different. Although difficult, she could count on her good health and was able to work. These were in and of themselves, enormous advantages. Therefore, we decided to ask our aunt to teach us how to use public transportation. She could also refer mother for work among the charitable people who had a stable financial situation.

The plan worked! Mother began to work cleaning houses, ironing and cooking for several families. Now, although our income was greater, the negative side was that mother had to spend all day outside of the house. Since I was the eldest, I picked up my siblings from grandma's house after school. Although this was a huge responsibility at my young age, I understood that the only chance we had to survive was by uniting. Consequently, I prepared the meals as best I could and took care of the kids while mother returned late in the evening. At one point, mother was working at two and three houses in a single day because this was her only option to generate additional income. Twelve hours of work for mother outside of our home became our new reality; nevertheless, we had to adapt so we would not die.

During weekends, my eight year-old brother and I started to go out with aunt Lico. While she begged for money, we learned to sell gum on the streets , in busses, and transportation terminals. An internal strength motivated us to continue on in spite of our weariness, even when sometimes we missed the bus that could take us back to our colony.

One day we decided to stay and sleep in a bus or train terminal during the weekend. That way we would not have to get up early because there was no school the next day. We would take turns during the night keeping watch so that the employees in these places would not find us sleeping and kick us out into the street. The terminal provided greater protection against the weather and evil people than if we were outside on the streets. We would also get on a bus that had the longest route, which allowed us to sleep several hours until dawn.

In the morning, we would take the route that took us home. Tired, hungry and sleep deprived but happy to have earned some money; we took advantage of our ride home to sell more gum and earn additional coins thus returning home with fuller pockets. In those pre-cell phone days, mother had no way of knowing where we were during our work hours. The big, concrete and noisy city made it impossible to try to find us and with even more fervor, mother asked God to protect us and bring us back home safely. On several occasions, God would send His angels who would guard us. During all of this time, amidst many dangers and often sleeping on the streets, we never encountered any significant mishaps.

Well aware of the dangers for a young adolescent girl, it occurred to me that I could dress as a boy by putting my hair inside a cap. I used wide pants and button down shirts for boys. This made such a convincing disguise that the other boys thought I was one of the guys. In this fashion I was able to meander, easily unnoticed, while avoiding serious dangers that I would not have been able to evade had they known my true identity. This strategy avoided the possibility of boys trying to go overboard with me and my brother having to fight in my defense. The most important aspect was our safety and we took care of each other. We never separated while we were on the street, knowing we could not depend on any adult.

Mother anxiously waited for our return. While she knew we were selling gum with our aunt, the perils were many and she continuously worried, knowing that at any given moment something could potentially befall us.

At home, our need was so great that we decided to continue pursuing our initiatives with my aunt's help every time we could. On weekends, mother made corn tortillas and my brother and I would also sell them outside of the local jail and also made special deliveries to wealthy people's houses. In time, I started to work as a baby sitter after I got out of school in the afternoon. This enabled me to earn more money and provide more support for our household than I could by selling gum. My sister Dioselina, the one that followed me, also learned to cook and take care of our siblings, taking on these responsibilities after school so I could work for pay elsewhere.

We all learned how to cooperate as a team and support the family in one way or another. We were motivated by love, without envy knowing that all of the money that came in was for all of us. Our goals were to protect the younger siblings, purchase food, and also medicines when we were ill.

Reflection

1. *Confronting that which apparently has no solution is a hard blow for an adult, and even more so for a child. After so much time I still held on to the illusion that I would find my father because it was too painful to accept that he had probably been killed. Had he disappeared for any other reason, we would have known.*

   This endless search took its toll on me, wearing my energy down, robbing me of sleep and causing me anxiety. After doing everything in our power, it is best to accept a loss, failure or pain, and learn to rest from it. To continue dreaming of impossibilities and illusions drains us, because the action arises from self-deceit which does not help us move forward but makes us stagnate. Is there anything in your history that does not let you move ahead? What is it?

2. *In different people, a similar situation can cause very different results. Aunt Lico is a fountain of inspiration because she overcame her limitations –which truly had few viable solutions– by taking on another approach. She did not remain submerged in her thoughts of impotence but exhausted her efforts, going after what was attainable. She sought in other people, potential solutions and alternatives that were not mere illusions and she was able to supply her family's basic needs. Are there any alternatives in your situation you may not be contemplating?*

3.   *Life is full of options and the key is to search and keep searching until you find them. If it is not possible through one route, perhaps another method will work. It is better to do something than to do nothing. What is stopping you? Are you ashamed? Are you fearful? Are you lazy? Or, do you feel incapable of doing something you have never attempted before? If you do not attempt something different than what you have been doing, you will never know the potential you have, nor the possibilities that await you.*

4.   *How do you confront difficulties in life? Do you stagnate while thinking, complaining and becoming bitter? Rather, have you tried seeking God, asking for His guidance and then proactively taking creative actions to overcome that which oppresses you? To a great degree, the results depend on you.*

5

CONFRONTING REALITY

I learned to fix my eyes on the future from my mother; to focus on what I could achieve, instead of burying myself in the past.

During this time, I crashed against the reality that we could only count on our limited income, and that my siblings depended solely on mother, on my brother Gabriel, and me. I had no other option than to help anyway I could. I was forced to grow up and mature at a young age. We had little sleep, because we spent many hours planning our activities for the next day to earn money and supply our innumerable needs. I would attend school sleep-deprived and often had nothing to eat for lunch. Today, I wonder if anyone noticed or if the majority of the time people are so entangled in themselves, that they don't perceive other people's needs.

Like all young ladies, I dreamt of buying fashion clothing, of going on vacation, eating what my friends brought to school and of my parents attending school meetings, like my other class mate's parents. I wanted my teachers to talk about my parents with pride, in front of the group, due to the contributions they made, like they did about other parents. However, my reality was the exact opposite. I felt like the girl with the tragic life, completely marginalized from society. I had no one I could ask for money to go on school events and trips and I knew mother only had enough for the basics; food, uniforms, school supplies, and shoes. For any additional expense, I had to be creative about how I could supply it. Nonetheless, if I spent resources on my personal desires, I would be contributing less to mother, thus the few decent clothing items I had were either purchased under a system similar to lay-away with weekly payments, or bought at second hand stores.

I understood that our goal was unity and the family's wellbeing. During that stage, I could have made many decisions that would have ruined our lives forever. I could have gotten involved with drugs or stolen items, just to get more money. However, mother taught us not just with words but also with her example. She always guided us with her good counsel; by making us aware of right and wrong actions and the consequences of each. She alerted us to avoid everything that is destructive.

Every day, I faced many challenges as well as new decisions. I remember that although I was young, I could chose not to do that which could negatively affect us, especially mother. I was a witness of how much she suffered and did not want to add to her pain. Consequently, I devoted myself to studying and working. Even so, at my age and in that environment like any adolescent, I felt tempted and was curious.

At times, I ditched classes with my friends for hours so we could go downtown. I did this on occasion to feel like I belonged to the group, not wanting to lose the little respect I had from my friends. They had become a strong influence over me and I sought to imitate them. Outside of my mother and siblings they were the only other people I had in my life. Today, I realize that an important element of prevention for my siblings and I from getting involved in vices, was that the people with whom we associated with were not involved in that kind of lifestyle.

A quality I had from an early age was that I was a day-dreamer. During recess, I used to sit near the school gardens imagining what I could become. I was passionate about singing and dreamed of being a famous movie star who would be on television. I thought that someday I could buy the clothes and shoes I wanted. I dreamt of marrying a good man and having a beautiful wedding. I would wear a long white dress and have an ideal home. I did not want to be ashamed when my friends visited me. We would live in a beautiful house and have a car.

Daydreaming helped me maintain a positive perspective and value myself as a woman while not letting any boy surpass the limits. I understood that nobody could protect me from the dangers of an unexpected pregnancy and it was my responsibility to make wholesome decisions. I was determined that in spite of peer pressures, I had dreams that gave meaning to all my sacrifice and weariness. I concluded that circumstances could snatch my father away but not my dreams.

In addition, I observed that each one of my brothers and sisters was suffering from some sort of ill treatment by their classmates. In the afternoons, we would get together to talk about the situations we had faced that day. In my brother Gabriel's situation, the mockery had escalated to such a degree that he felt obliged to abandon school in the fifth grade. Although mother sent him to class, he would go to grandmother's house to wait untill it was time to return home. While attending parent-teacher conferences one day, mother caught on to what was happening, but by then he was too far behind to catch up with school work. She decided to sign him up for adult night classes, which was also for youth who had missed several school years. Unfortunately, this did not work either.

Although the teasing also affected the girls in my family, we seemed to handle it better. Besides, they were not as cruel as with my brother who as a young man would respond violently when his pride was wounded. Gabriel was raised on the street, without a healthy father figure to guide and defend him. When the other kids insulted him, my brother would punch them or yell back offensively to defend himself.

Despite many difficulties and sacrifices, I finally graduated from high school. I had many dreams and the enthusiasm to continue my education, yet we did not have sufficient resources to make it a reality. In spite of it all, life began to improve, especially for the little ones. Together we were able to overcome many other difficulties.

Mother continued working literally from sun up to sun down. Even with all of this effort, our funds were not enough to build our own larger house because we had to cover education related expenses for seven children, in a country where education is not free.

My mother

Something that impacted me during this time was that I never heard mother curse despite her recognizing that father was responsible for the majority of mishaps to which we had succumbed. However, in spite of the pain his abandonment had caused us I always heard her praying to God for him and teaching us to pray in like manner. In spite of all the hard work she had to perform, once she understood she could no longer depend on father, she never gave up. It was customary for us to wake up at dawn. She would make breakfast, then wash and get us ready for school, before she left for work. When she arrived home at night, her hands always carried food and she would have us all sit at the table and share adequate portions for everyone.

During our meals, I remember her saying, "My sons and daughters, I love you very much, and I want you to know that although I may not see you during the entire day, you are in my thoughts and prayers frequently. I want you to lack nothing."

She gave us an affectionate kiss, before going to sleep, through which she transmitted her love, abnegation and commitment. She treated us equally, without favoritisms and would rather not eat than let us go hungry. She would celebrate our birthdays with a small cake that she asked our neighbor to make, and with her joy and jokes she would make us laugh and have a good time.

Although she was out of the house the entire day she would be very much engaged in our lives, knowing our friends, what we were doing and if we had had any problems. Her life consisted of working and caring of us. She gave us all the love she could and would discipline us when needed. She never lacked food on the one hand and correction on the other. I thank God for having given me an irreproachable mother. To a great degree, all of us are who we are today because of her.

From mother I learned to fix my eyes on the future and focus on what I could achieve instead of burying myself in the past. Mother did not sit and watch life pass her by; instead she made a covenant with God requesting He sustain her so she would not relent when facing obstacles, no matter how big they were. I believe the most valuable aspect mother passed on to us was to love and trust God.

Today, I understand that circumstances do not have to be perfect to achieve what we desire. It is the struggles themselves, and the use of our skills, what grow and develop us in every circumstance. Mother taught us a lot about love and mutual sacrifice in a family. She also taught us to wrestle with situations until we obtained victory. We learned to not see ourselves as victims and to never give up when facing obstacles.

The years passed along without any news of father. Then, some of mother's brothers who lived in the United States offered us their support by inviting her to immigrate to The United States. This way it would be easier for her to provide for our needs.

Mother had never separated from us, and it was a difficult decision she had to make because of the increasing expenses associated with growing children. We believed the option to immigrate was a good opportunity for the family because it offered us a better future. Thus, she planned her trip and communicated this to us. I gave my full support, fully aware of the situation.

When mother left for the United States, I was 14 and remained behind in charge of my four siblings while my maternal grandmother, who still lived in the ranch, cared for the two youngest –the 2 and 3 years olds. It was difficult to depart to work so far away, not knowing what could befall us. Nevertheless, courage and love helped her make the decision. Our farewell to mother marked another gray day in our history. I have no recollection of that day. Perhaps because my grief was so intense, I unintentionally erased it from my mind.

While caring for my siblings, I continued attending school during the day and working in the evenings. I would arrive home at night and help them with what they needed. In the interim, Dioselina, who was 12 years old, would prepare the meals and clean the house. We all maintained our normal routines; though we felt that life without mother was empty and sad.

Another year passed since her departure. I remember that before going to bed, my siblings would ask when mother would be back and why she was no longer with us. My sister and I would explain she was working far, far away, to give us a better life. Yet the explanations did not diminish the sadness in their faces. My sister Dioselina and I were practically the mothers of these little ones and they would seek us out to feel protected.

Our relatives would visit, on occasion; however, none of them came to live with us. Our sorrow grew with time. None of us wanted to live far away from mother and while we spoke by phone and wrote to each other, it was not enough.

One day, uncle Victorino –mother's brother who was on his way to the United States– came to see us. He asked if we wanted to send pictures or letters to mother, since he would soon be going to where she was living. That very instant it occurred to me that I could travel to the U.S. with him and continue the search for father, which had not been resolved in my soul. I wanted to look for father personally as well as continue working to help mother out. Initially, my idea was that with my help we could return home faster.

I mentioned the idea to my siblings and we concluded that it was a good idea. Dioselina, then 13, would care for the younger siblings. My uncle did not initially agree, but finally, I convinced him.

I called mother to consult with her about what I wanted to do .She said she did not agree with my plans and that she would soon be back with us. Inside of me there was this profound fear and the recurring thought that the same thing that happened to father could happen to her. I was tormented with thoughts of never seeing her again, yet at the same time I was conscious of the dangers to which illegal immigrants were exposed to when crossing the border. On the other hand, I had learned to take care of myself on the streets of Morelia. The thought of being with mother again in order to plan our return to Mexico and reunite our family, dominated me.

Therefore, I used my persuasive skills and in spite of mother's opposition, convinced uncle Victorino to let me go with him. I told him that when she saw me she would be very happy. Besides, he and I had grown up together, and we had mutual trust. One week later, I left the city with uncle Victorino and Israel, one of mother's cousins. I was 15 and they were in their early twenties.

Reflection

1. *Your decisions... your decisions, your decisions... Everything you do has consequences, whether positive or negative. Not only for you, but also for those around you. Your decisions affect those whom you love and even those whom you do not know (such as future children, spouses, and grandchildren...) You can plant and build up or pull down and destroy through decisions that are not submitted to a balanced analysis and looked at from different angles.*

   Above all, decisions that do not contemplate God's principles are eventually destined to fail. What pending decisions are you currently facing that could change your future? Have you consulted your Maker concerning the best method, person or timing to respond to that situation?

2. *One of the people that can most influence our life is our mother. Some mothers kill their children with terrible personal examples, with condemning words or with abuse, leaving them forever wounded. Other mothers may not abandon their children physically, yet they do so emotionally or by leaving them to bear the weight of their worst decisions.*

On the other hand, some mothers make decisions that bring health and happiness to their children. My mother was self-sacrificing, disciplined, and loving. She refused to give up when challenged by exhaustion, problems and discouragement. How was your mother? Which of her decisions strengthened, encouraged, and guided you towards positive outcomes? Which ones hurt you?

3. *What kind of mother or father are you, or will you be? Have you thought about how your decisions today will affect your children tomorrow? How will they affect your spouse... extended family... friends?*

6

THE THIRD ABANDONMENT

> *Oh how much pain and damage we were causing all these little ones; without realizing it or wanting to.*

I will never forget the night before I left. We all sat down in our small room that had no furniture other than a bed which we all shared and talked for a long time. We looked like important executives discussing our plans. I told my siblings I would be leaving Mexico the next day and did not know when I would see them again.

Dioselina would have utterly shocked any adult. She was a strong and courageous child who almost immediately assumed the new challenge, ready to take on any necessary tasks. Right after mother's departure she had taken charge of administrating the little funds we had to purchase supplies. Dioselina was an adult in a child's body who was very responsible and organized.

Truthfully, I was the one who frequently wanted to over spend, thinking I would replace the funds by working. Not only did Dioselina accomplish the administrative tasks, she also cooked and washed the clothing. From a very young age she was a wonderful administrator and homemaker. When mother left, she became a great help for me. She was now willing to continue doing everything with Gabriel's help.

Gabriel and I had bonded quite a lot because we worked together. At the age of 8, he would buy our daily milk and bread. Now he was distraught to learn I would not be there any longer to keep working side by side with him. To a great degree, Gabriel depended on me while at the same time he took care of me. He had become a father to all of us though he was still a child.

Elia, who was the next eldest, was like a real life doll. I experimented on her all kinds of hair styles and fashions while she, innocent and beautiful, would let me do whatever I wanted. I dressed her, colored her nails and took her for walks at the mall. When I had a little extra money I would buy her something small, even though it was not necessarily what she wanted. She was content with my promise that someday we would have enough to buy her the dolls she desired. Israel, the sibling that followed Elia, was too small to understand what was going on. The only thing he knew was that his other mother was also leaving him to go work far away. This time, he was not willing to allow it and as soon as we told him, he ran and hugged my feet repeating, "Please don't leave me mama!"

Oh how much pain and damage we were causing all these little ones without realizeng it or wanting to. Inside in their memory, we were making profound prints of abandonment and lack of love which is how a child interprets these departures.

"Why does everyone I love leave," a little one asks. "Is it because I am misbehaving?" They may not use the same words, however these feelings are present and children are the ones who pay the greatest cost of an adult's decisions since they cannot advocate for themselves. Time would show our family how these episodes of abandonment affected our youngest siblings.

I knew that although I could explain my reasons, Israel would not understand them. I assured him that mother and I would never stop loving him and hugged him for a long time until he fell asleep. Elena and Alma, the youngest girls, continued living with grandmother Zenaida at the ranch. We used to visit them during school vacations, when we would bring them clothes and shoes and then return to the city, leaving them heartbroken when we departed.

My contradicting emotions did not allow me to sleep. I was anxious because of the trip and worried about leaving my siblings alone. I was also scared, thinking something could happen to me along the way and that I might not be able to see them or mother again. On the other hand, I was overjoyed thinking I would reunite with mother. I wanted to hug her tightly and begin working to buy my siblings all the things I had promised them. At 15, I also felt ready to face a new world after the trip we would be making the following day. My dreams for my family propelled me and minimized fears of tragedies I had heard of and fear of the unknown.

My Farewell

In the morning, before they awoke, I kissed them one by one and left with my uncles to go to the bus terminal. I took an old backpack, some clothing and a few pictures of my siblings so I could see their faces all the time. We climbed on the bus that would take us to the border and I sat near the window most of the trip, quietly observing what I was leaving behind. Nostalgia enveloped me. As we slowly moved away, I felt as if my soul was disintegrating and I was slowly perishing. I was leaving behind what had been my entire life and a great portion of it was my siblings whom I wholeheartedly loved.

At times I cried, while other times I smiled thinking that maybe I would find father. Many years had passed, yet I still could not accept his disappearance. I had the hope that I was going to find him. This desire was a strong motivator that helped me embark on this new journey.

The crossing was long, some sixteen hours by bus. I had lots of time to think and face my own feelings. At times I felt I was literally dying of sadness; however, the desire to reach my goals was just as strong and they propelled me to look forward and not stagnate in my today, and much less in my yesterdays.

Finally, we reached the border and stayed for the night in a hotel. We called mother, who was in California, and although she was very upset that I was with my uncles, at the same time she was very happy she would see me again. No doubt, she felt lonely without any of her children. She also knew she could count on me and we would team up well together.

My uncles had contacted the same person that helped them cross the border into California before. The next day, we began the journey at night encountering all types of difficulties during the next three days. We were not carrying enough food or water because it was heavy and we needed to travel lightly to move with agility. The first obstacles we had to overcome were bushes that cut into our skin. They stung and crossing throught them required courage and determination for us to continue. In my mind, at times I wanted to cry and even turn back. I remembered what they told us about what happened to "wet backs," and I knew I was exposing myself to rape or even death. Nevertheless, I focused my faith on God and not on negative scenarios.

On the border between Mexico and the U.S., many people have died following their dream. Though my heart beat rapidly, I did not demonstrate fear when having to jump fences or cross rivers. These rivers, though small, were murky and dirty with all kinds of animals both visible and microscopic and the infections that travelers acquired frequently took their lives. I knew of people who had to drink their own urine when they were unable to find water.

In our case, we walked all night long trying to advance as much as possible. I wanted to stop and rest, my feet were hurting and I felt I would collapse because I was so tired. Nonetheless, our instructions were that we could not stop because if we did, we would expose ourselves and it would be easier for the border police to spot us during the day. I would encourage myself by repeating internally, "We're almost there... we're going to do this... we are getting closer." I sought to distract my mind and not think about the negative aspects or the fear I was feeling.

Morning finally came, and we had arrived. Nights were extremely cold in the dessert and intensely hot during the day. The dessert's penetrating heat caused an almost unbearable thirst. We felt as if we were dying of thirst, but there was little water. Besides, we had to share it and it was so hot we felt as if we were choking. There in that place, hardly anything grew. It was inhospitable for human beings and even for animals. In a dessert the heat is so unbearable that one cannot think. Even your thoughts feel fried with the sun's forceful rays. How I longed for some shade in a place where my skin, wounded by the bushes would not sting as much. Nevertheless, we had to wait there for the train that would take us to our final destination.

When the train finally arrived, we quickly climbed onboard as there was little time. I had to enter through a small opening in the back of a wagon. One of my uncles was staying in front of the opening so I wouldn't fall out with the train's bumps. To be able to fit in, I had to roll my body completely into a ball which severely restricted my breathing, but there was no other option. At some point during the journey I screamed desperately, telling my uncles that I could no longer stand it. They encouraged me to go on,in spite of feeling that the ride would never end.

The train advanced rapidly and I was dying to get out, yet it was not possible until it stopped. I decided to cry out to God for help and strength. I was conscious and told myself I did not want to die there in that train and I hung on to life, inhaling what little air I could get. After a long time, the train slowed down. A certain hope that I would be able to get out of there alive, invaded me. Then, I heard my uncle's and the voices of the others who were helping us across. They said immigration was close and they had seen us. They told me to stay still and not speak. The train came to a complete halt in the middle of the dessert. The sun flashed its rays with maximum potency and I was perspiring not just due to the heat, but due to fear. My uncle did not move until the men got closer and told us to get out.

My uncle had warned me that if they did not seen me, I should not come out. At least I would not be trapped, even if they were found out. My fears escalated and I did not want to be left alone. Besides, I had been asking God for the train to stop soon as I did not feel I could hold out much longer in that position. Because I was sufficating, it was a relief to camo out. The immigration officer was kind and helped me get down. My fears subsided when I saw that although we were taken to a police station where we were interrogated, they also treated us humanely. They gave us sandwiches made from cold cuts and cheese, which we devoured without complaints. The next day, they deported us and took us to the border in Mexicali.

My hope challenged

I was overcome by sadness once again. We had returned to the family's house that was helping us cross the border. What frustration! Now, when would we be able to see mother? When would I find father? With this terrible experience vividly in my mind, I could not stop thinking of what I had felt. I felt fear and anguish knowing we had come close to losing our lives. Hungry, tired and thirsty we were also utterly exhausted. I resisted thinking we would have to repeat the journey we had been through in an attempt to cross all over again. I felt so desperate that I proposed my uncles send me back to Morelia. However, this was no longer an option.

That night, we rested in luxury. I was in a comfortable bed with a fan. There, they fed us good-tasting, hot, fresh food. I felt like I had come back to life. During the next four days, while we tried to cross the border once more we could not speak via the telephone with mother or my siblings. I was dejected and depressed. In spite of this, the longing to reunite with mother gave me the courage I needed to attempt to cross one more time.

The anticipated day arrived and we began our journey towards the border. This time it was not any better or easier than the first. When we got to the other side, on North American soil, we slept under a bridge. We took turns sleeping so that no one would steal the few items of clothing and food we were carrying. During my turn on guard, I was surprised by the reptiles that had previously traumatized me. There were snakes threatening to enter the area where we were resting. However, arming myself with courage I threw rocks that scared them away.

During the trip, our diet consisted of white bread and water. Everything was rationed so even if we were hungry we needed to hold out. There was just a little for everyone, just enough to derive strength to keep going until we reached our destination. We took the same route as the previous time, walking the path that led to the train and then we mounted it once again. I felt that same paralyzing fear as I thought of the asphyxiating ride, yet at the same time I had faith we would achieve our goal this time. Happily, on this occasion, the conductor did not see us hop on and did not stop. Besides the heat, thirst and hunger we had no other obstacles. We were three days on the road, three days, walking without stopping until the last night.

Before dawn, a truck finally picked us up and took us to a mobile home to rest. How I longed to rest, stretch and relax my battered muscles. I wanted to enter into a deep sleep to alleviate my weariness, but I couldn't as I felt somewhat nervous and was anxious to see mother. Several times I asked what time we were going to arrive, but my uncles wanted to sleep and requested I stop inquiring so much and just go to sleep.

I lay there in silence but awake, imagining the moment I would again see mother. Very early the next day, they took us to where we finally met up with her and I was able to hug my dear mother! I had not felt that happy in a long time. We cried for a while even as mother caressed my face and hugged me for some time. She was surprised at my courage to cross the border since she never imagined I would be able to do it. We were both ecstatic and she had taken the day off to spend time with me.

The next day, my first awakening in the United States, was a surprise for me and was the start of a new stage of my life. Almost nothing was as I had dreamed it and even more completely different than how travelers had described it! People who had lived in the United States would return to my country relaying their very favorable experiences. Now I felt betrayed! I had purchased a new outfit to wear on my first day in the US, thinking that all people dressed well here and I did not want to look ridiculous. I thought all of the houses were large and luxurious and that there was no trash on the streets or poverty like there was in Mexico. The image in my mind turned out to be a fantasy from which I soon woke up.

A New Language and Customs Along With New Rejections

The house in which mother lived only had two bedrooms, with a living room and a kitchen so small that two people could not fit in it at the same time. My Aunt Adela –my mother's sister– with her husband and four children, her brother-in-law, my mother and of course, now me, nine people, all lived there. The first thing that mother said was, "Wake up early, if you want to take a shower. Otherwise, you will have to wait a long time. After you shower, we will go to the store, by foot, to buy something to eat as a complement to breakfast. Then, we will go wash the clothes."

Many questions invaded my mind. What is this? Where did I arrive? Wasn't I going to the United States, the great country where no one lacks anything? Didn't people have all of the commodities they wanted there?

So what is this about going to wash clothes? I could not believe it! I thought surely someone washed your clothes and all you did was dedicate yourself to work and go to school. What illusions had I forged? Undoubtedly, I had done so with the help of travelers that using elaborate and exaggerated tales had told us of so many wonders. Moreover, this was only the beginning. From then on, everything worsened.

The positive aspect, I thought, was that I was finally close to mother again and could look for father. She was the only other reason I had travelled to this country. Nonetheless, that illusion also soon burst and the reality was that I only saw her a few minutes in the morning before she went to work and a few more in the afternoon while we had dinner. She worked 10 hour shifts in a hotel, cleaning rooms and was exhausted when she finished her shift.

I also crashed against another wall. Because I was only 15 years old it was difficult to find a job and though I wanted to go to school, the main reason I had travelled to America had not been to study. I wanted to work and help mother save money so we could return to our country sooner. As far as searching for father, I had no idea where to begin, or who to ask, other than our family. We lived closer to father's bothers, yet my uncles were always busy with their own problems, obligations, and children and they did not have time to think about father –to whom they referred to as irresponsible– and his disappearance. When I asked for help to look for him, they replied with cruel remarks about him all which just made me even sadder. They had their children beside them and I soon understood the message they were transmitting, as well as their lack of understanding and interest in our case. With time, I stopped asking for their help.

Not long after I arrived, some friends asked if I wanted to babysit. I accepted, to stay at their place and sleep there during the week and return home with mother on weekends. However, mother also worked during weekends. Our lack of time together, and scarce dialogue made our relationship colder.

Months flew by quickly and my life was both monotonous and sad. I missed my siblings and friends, as well as the culture of my country. I was so depressed I could not sleep well, but I could not see other options. I had been sociable and tried to go to social gatherings with my uncles to meet new people. However, none of the new girls wanted to be my friends. I think it had to do with the fact I didn't speak English and when I tried to establish a conversation with girls my age, they would either leave or ignore me. They would look at me and treat me like a stranger. I felt like an extraterrestrial being, out side of their world and always alone in some corner thinking about my siblings. I found myself alone or talking with adults most of the time. Without realizing it, I became rebellious towards mother and other adults. My attitude began to destroy the ties of friendship and respect that had united us for years. I was always motherless on weekends until finally I was able to work in a taco stand near our house. There, I met a girl who was older than me and we started what soon became a close friendship. She became very special to me and her influence was evident when I decided to go out dancing to night clubs with her, behind mother's back.

Because mother was always so tired and went to sleep early in the evening I took advantage of this to leave with my friend. The worst thing was that I started to lie to mother telling her that I had to work late, when I was really out with her somewhere. When mother found out about this friendship she expressed her disagreement because at age nineteen, this girl already had two children from different fathers. My friend was also rebellious with her mother and would leave her children for her to take care of while she was out having fun.

When mother prohibited me from being this girl's friend, the first thing that crossed my mind was that mother had become quite selfish and was no longer on my side. It seemed like she wanted to kill me with boredom, pushing me away from my new best friend. She constantly criticized my friends, whom I considered to be my new family. From my myopic perspective, I defended them from her criticism and it was offensive to me that she believed they were having a bad influence on me.

I couldn't understand the reasons why mother would not allow me to go out with the girls who, according to me, only wanted what was best for me. I did not see the dangers or perceive the way I was changing. I was completely blinded against mother's warnings and I decided that if I just worked, I could give her money during the weekend, which would keep her happy. I thought she would let me go out without reproach and I wanted to buy my independence from mother at any cost. Nevertheless, I did not know how wrong I was! I ended up paying for each one of my acts of rebellion against mother with the treason and pain that my beloved friends caused me.

At the end, mother was proved right. Though I caused her many problems and tears she never turned her back on me or stopped loving me. Even when I realized I was to blame for my rebellion and was suffering from the consequences and disappointments, she always had encouraging words that I did not know how to value.

After several months, the knocks of life continued striking me ever stronger to waken and bring me to consciousness. I considered getting a fresh start and regaining lost time. I was aware that the reality of poverty and need that my brothers and sisters still lived in had become a very distant one for me. I had lived in the U.S. for one year and I did not feel I was fulfilling the objectives for which I had come.

Then mother spoke with a few of father's brothers that lived near Los Angeles, which was five hours from where we were and asked them to allow me to live with them, in order to better meet my goals. I took a bus, once again distancing myself from mother and arrived to live with father's sister, who had resided in the U.S. most of her life. I had only seen her a few times when she traveled to Mexico on vacation. She lived in an even smaller one-bedroom apartment. She shared her roof with two daughters, two nephews and now me. I was assigned to sleep in the closet, where they all stored their belongings. It was large and I fit in there perfectly. I did not complain about this. On the contrary, I now felt like I had my own space. My father's other brothers, who were nearby, helped me find a job.

I felt freer now, thinking that this stage, far from mother, would work well. I thought of myself as an adult and of course, I knew everything now. I would not have mother's boring advice, her words of precaution, her fears or reproaches; rather, I would govern my life alone.

However, I soon began to miss her and my siblings. While I was away from mother, I became more aware of my actions and I repented of having caused her pain. Even after I allowed my friends to influence me to commit so much foolishness, I was desirous to make something of myself. I wanted to change my life and the lives of my siblings. Once again, I refocused my thoughts towards the path I wanted to follow. Five months later, mother also came to live with my aunt and we shared the closet space together.

Since I now felt settled into the new city, I decided to take advantage of social gatherings to learn English. It occurred to me that to help grasp the language, I could talk to little kids and with my new friends, asking them how to say this and that word. I began to lose my fear of using the language and started attending night school while working during the day in a factory. With all of these good changes, I still felt empty and sad; nothing gave me a sense of fulfillment.

Unfortunately, the situation worsened. This adolescent stage was full of turmoil for me just as it is for so many other youths. I was undergoing difficult changes, from various angles. I was adjusting to a new country with a new culture and a different language. I was far away from my immediate family and the family with whom we now lived, I did not really know well. Above all, the normal adolescent changes generated confusion within me. I felt none of my goals were realistic and I was just limiting myself to existing, with little purpose in life other than to work, eat and sleep.

Although I was grateful for all I now had and was learning to seek positive angles in life, I knew that to focus on the work routine would not help me strive for my dreams and for what I wanted to achieve.

Reflection

1. The majority of adolescents believe that to be independent is equivalent to being free! They consider that to be free means being able to do what ever they want, when they want, and with whom they want, without considering the other side of the coin, which are the consequences of each of their actions.

    I have understood that freedom begins by learning to accept oneself; whether you think you are pretty, not pretty, have sports abilities or not, possess money or lack it... with or without a father. Have you learned to accept yourself? Do you really understand that everything you decide has at least one and most likely several consequences for you and those around you?

2. *Freedom does not just have a physical dimension. It implies assuming responsibility for freedom of your thoughts, and freedom of your actions. You are responsible for your sexuality, and how you use your body, how you use your time and how you manage your money. How are you doing in each one of these areas? In which ones do you need further preparation? Remember, you may not know something today, but everything in life can be learned or unlearned.*

3. *What is freedom for you? Describe it. Remember that freedom comes with responsibilities and you will enjoy it to the degree you make responsible choices. In which ways are you assuming your freedoms and your responsibilities? If you believe you have no responsibilities, you are moving in a car without breaks that sooner, rather than later, will crash! That dear reader, is poor use of your freedom!*

7

LOW SELF-ESTEEM

Your manner of perceiving a situation allows you to have the battle half won or half lost.

My low self-esteem was evident. It was like a darkness inside of me and it made me feel fearful and insecure whenever I thought about what others were expecting of me. I worried about what people thought about me, how they would judge me, what they could say to me and ultimately, what they said to each other about me. This feeling was destroying my dreams and goals. But how could I change my low self-esteem? With time, I identified that my negative thoughts were my main enemies and if I wanted to do something with my life it would require me to start by changing my way of thinking.

I started by deciding I was not going to allow obstacles to defeat me. A popular saying states that whether you think you can, or think you can't, you are right. Your manner of perceiving a situation allows you to have the battle either half won or half lost. It all depends on you. Part of this radical change occurs when we learn to be grateful and stop complaining for that which we feel we lack. We can start by facing a mirror, speaking to ourselves and saying, "Besides being beautiful, I am intelligent and possess wonderful abilities that I can give this world."

Though I did not have a strong relationship with God, I began to connect with and thank Him for all the opportunities He was providing that were allowing me to grow, learn and love. This introspective view drove me to understand that I needed to love myself and other people. My current circumstances whether good or bad, were not what defined me. What was important was what I did with each one of them. I was learning to enjoy every day with an attitude focused on the good and the beautiful things around me. When you live this way, you start learning to triumph daily.

Though I was the social type, I grew up facing so much rejection and criticism that it drove me to feel inferior to other people. However, mother's lessons and those of a few friends who understood that every human being has a purpose, helped me to focus on goals that gave my existence meaning and courage. My family, people with faith in God and my growing trust in myself, helped me understand that no one could rob me of my dreams if I did not allow it.

For several years, I struggled with my feelings of inferiority and rejection daily. I had to prove to myself that I was capable of achieving what I proposed. This battle, for me or for anyone else that is in a similar situation is not easy. It requires facing constant challenges, putting on the armor of faith and courage and trying different tasks and activities. You will ultimately find that which comes naturally to you, or that you can do well and enjoy. It is vital to try repeatedly, until you reach your goals. This process positively escalates our self-esteem.

With my mother's help, I overcame this stage. During those days when I began a dialogue with God, she would help me face my fears. Mother was a woman of faith and taught me what she had learned and put into practice.

I did not have a masculine figure in my life, since mother did not remarry for fear of bringing another man into the house that could harm us. Not having to adapt to another male in our life was something positive, but on the other hand I lacked the love and acceptance of a father figure. This element contributed negatively in my formative years causing me to become rebellious. In spite of this, I received encouragement from people I knew who recognized I was a young woman with many dreams.

Discovering My Talents

With so many financial difficulties, most of my childhood dreams of wanting to sing and act started to dissipate, especially because I still focused my energy on helping mother support my siblings. One day, I had the opportunity to participate in a singing contest at a local restaurant, which would be televised. Knowing of my musical inclination, which I had inherited from father, my uncles took me there.

Although I almost withdrew because of my low self-esteem, I finally participated and enjoyed sharing the time with other talented people. For the first time in my life, I realized I had achieved something I really enjoyed. I won the contest, tying with another child my age, and the prize was $1,000 dollars, which was more than I earned in one month's worth of work. I received an invitation to sing with a local group that played at sporting events and on several occasions I participated with them.

During one of these events, my friends introduced me to the manager of some well-known international musical groups. I shared with him my passion for singing and he was interested in helping me. He connected me with people in that media; however, the opportunity required me to appear live in Los Angeles, where the recording studios, as well as the people that would coach me were located. When mother heard the proposal, she felt that at age 15 I was not mature enough to go live on my own. She could not abandon her job to come with me, because my siblings were still small and depended on us. With all of the pain in my heart, I let that opportunity go, although I thought it was not fair. I awoke from the dream once again to my sad reality and continued working, because this was the reason I had come to the United States.

There are occasions when we miss opportunities to do what we enjoy most, yet later I discovered it would perhaps not have been the best thing for me at that age. However, at the end of the competition participating with the group helped me develop and grow my self-esteem and personal security. I felt assured in such a way that I was able to continue facing the challenges that, without a doubt would come into my life. I also learned to continue defending what I think, as well as my dreams, which define and strengthen us for a lifetime.

No wonder they call boyfriend in Spanish, the "Did-not-see"

In the midst of these changes, I never forgot father. One of the reasons I had agreed to live with father's sister was that I thought she could help me find him, or perhaps she had more information about him. Nonetheless, their lifestyle was no different from mother's brothers; each one was enveloped in their own routine. Shortly after having moved to my aunt's, I made new friends. Among them, I met a young man, the brother of one of these friends. He was fun and I enjoyed his company. With time, we engaged in a relationship about which I did not tell my aunts or mother. By that time, mother had come to live with us and I feared she would not approve of me seeing him.

Mother continued being what I considered extremely over protective and did not allow me to go out alone anywhere. When I finally mentioned I had a friend, she worried. She did not want me to get too excited about my admirer, so that later I would not be disappointed. She suspected we were "novios" (which in Spanish literally means did not see), or as we'd say in English, "going steady," but I concealed it from her. I didn't think I was doing anything wrong.

My attitude and self-esteem were improving, yet I was still an inexperienced, naive and myopic adolescent. As the Spanish saying goes, "The devil knows more due to his age, than to his wickedness." I did not have mother's years to understand life better. Again, I felt as if mother wanted to isolate me from the world and that, I considered selfish. The relationship with this young man once again created a barrier between mother and myself. Today, I understand how blind I was. I was searching for the paternal affection that I lacked, in this young man. Beside him, I felt some of that protection that I had not had for several years. Though I did not understand it, mother only wanted to protect me from failure. In my naiveté, I judged her without understanding that her overprotection was a result of her immense love for me.

Against all of her opposition, I secretly continued going out with my boyfriend. I had a close relationship with his sisters and went to see them almost on a daily basis. I was pleased with how warmly and kindly they treated me and soon I felt like part of the family that I didn't feel I had. Mother knew them and thought they were good people. She had seen my boyfriend a few times, but didn't like his demeanor or how he dressed. She considered him a youth without goals or clear objectives. One day, he came to drop me off at the apartment where we lived. Mother was outside waiting for me. When we stepped out of the car, he said he would like to speak with her; however, in a firm tone mother declined and asked that he leave me alone. As he left, I swelled up with anger.

I thought I would never see him again. I was full of fear because in spite of mother's opinion, I thought he was a good man for me who made me feel important and protected. I didn't want to stop seeing him; he had become a well-entrenched whim. I locked myself in the closet where we both slept while thousands of thoughts whirled through my head. Outside, she spoke with my aunts about the occurrence and gave clear instructions they should never again allow this boy to come near me. She confirmed with my aunts that we would soon be returning to Mexico.

I knew that at least in part, mother depended on me to help her raise my siblings by contributing the money I earned. However, I was blinded by my feelings towards that boy. Mother had goals and dreams for my life, but she couldn't find a way to communicate and transmit her feelings. I had shut her off. She was timid and at that point we were no longer talking nor discussing my adolescent changes and development as a woman even less. These types of conversations made her feel embarrassed, and what I was learning about my emotions I had to face alone. My friends' counsel, to be frank, was not the most appropriate. The night my mother decided to separate me from my boyfriend permanently, I waited for the best moment and when no one was expecting it, I escaped from the apartment at night. I told myself that I was ready to start my own family and be free from mother.

While this was going on, my siblings were still living alone in Mexico, under the care of Dioselina. The two youngest girls were still at the ranch with grandma, waiting for our return. We wrote letters and spoke on the phone once or twice a month. We would send them clothing, shoes and other personal care items through special mail carrier services. In spite of the distance, we truly loved them. However, the fact that we didn't see them and were immersed in another reality so far away caused us to start to lose that connection we had had while I was living in Mexico. Each time we talked, we had less to talk about and each person was heading their separate way as they developed new friendships and different interests.

Reflection

My low self-esteem was not resolved immediately. It took years until I learned to value my qualities, and also to recognize my weaknesses. Discovering my singing talent and other personal strengths helped me gain confidence in what I was capable of doing and achieving. However, the process took time, while I tried different activities to discover who I was.

The maturing process, which implies time, brought me to a juncture where I made unfavorable decisions, but I didn't know that I lacked a balanced perception of myself. After many mistakes, I started to acquire personal security and learned to treat others better because I began to feel better about myself. How do you treat others? Don't you think this is a direct reflection of how you feel about yourself?

8

FREE... FREE AT LAST!

The story does not always have a fairy tale ending

The night I fled from what I considered my far from ideal home, I was looking for a new destiny. I walked along the street thinking about what I wanted to do with my life. The truth is, I wasn't sure if I wanted to go after my boyfriend or not. While I walked, I heard the sound of a horn from an approaching car behind me. Surprised, I turned and saw my boyfriend. He was driving near where I lived and hoped to see me outside. I took this as a sign of destiny, rather than a trap along the way. Without much thought, I left with him to his apartment where we would start our new life together.

We agreed that I would live with him from that moment on. I was only seventeen and he was twenty-three. At this young age, I did not clearly understand the meaning of commitment. I also lacked understanding about loyalty and the implications and responsibilities of a home. We had not spoken about essential elements to avoid failure in a relationship, nor had I seen such an example at my parent's home. No one had ever explained the importance of these things to me, not even at school. The only thing we could think about was that we would both work, which would enable us to easily pay for rent. What blindness and narrowness of thought not to be able to see beyond our noses the reality before us!

I still dreamed of a wedding with a white gown in a large church, surrounded by my family. However, when this situation came along I completely forgot my original plan, thinking that perhaps this was my destiny and later on, I would be able to pick up my plan where I had left off. Now, the important thing was to fight so I wouldn't lose this man who was offering me a home, a new life and freedom.

As was to be expected, being an immature adolescent who had no idea of the implications of this kind of union, it was not easy for me to start a life with another person that was just as or even more immature than me, who was not ready to assume the challenges of being a family. For me, as for many women, it was like being in a fairy tale. After so much suffering, the princess had found her Prince Charming. Now, nothing and no one could come between them and they would live happily ever after.

However, the story doesn't always have a fairy tale ending, like we all hope. In the beginning, it was lots of fun. We were both young and had good intentions. We had both been raised far away from our fathers and believed this new relationship gave us the opportunity to correct the mistakes we had experienced in our parent's homes. No one had prepared us to assume this relationship, but as the inexperienced usually think, we already knew everything.

A new destiny? Time took care of bursting that bubble and showing us the multiple challenges of a living together type relationship. In my case, I had to behave like a mature woman and assume the responsibilities of a home. The honeymoon soon dissipated and our personalities soon surfaced, with each of us acting as if we were still single, failing to take the needs of the other into consideration. For me, while I lived with mother she reserved a portion of money from my check which she would give me at the end of the week so I could buy what I wanted. Now, I could not do that; all of the money I earned I had to use to pay the new bills and obligations we were acquiring. I also could not give mother the same amount of money I had been giving her before.

I had never contemplated the ramifications of this and it made me feel bad because I knew that my siblings needed the funds. It was not long before I realized what I had done; but my pride refused to let me go back on the decision I had made. Although I wanted to, I did not have the courage to tell mother I wanted to return, because I felt ashamed. I realized my leaving her had not just caused her pain, but offended her and damaged our relationship even more. At times I wanted to run and ask for her forgiveness; however, I did not feel worthy of her. I knew that mother would not have thought twice about taking me back in, but I had also dishonored my entire family. I decided to continue living with my boyfriend, despite my being full of remorse.

My boyfriend had a lifestyle that generated friction in the relationship. He would go out every weekend and party with his friends. He would arrive home at dawn, without it even occurring to him that I needed some sort of explanation. He also had no awareness of the need to be accountable. In those early days, I would go out with him and see his friends get drunk, but I didn't feel comfortable in that environment. I quickly got to the point where I preferred to wait for him at home.

The waiting seemed like a time without end. Sometimes he didn't even come back home, choosing to sleep at his friends' house. My struggle was not with another woman, but with other habits. The next day, we would have a great big fight over his outings. He would say that when I had gone to live with him I knew he liked partying and drinking. While he was right, he could not understand that we had assumed a new life together and this meant we were supposed to take each other into consideration and make decisions together, not separately as if we were still single. Besides, he did not understand that I had left my family, abandoned my dreams and betrayed my siblings for him. It was painful to see he didn't care about anything I was feeling and focused only on what made him happy.

Mother had told me he didn't seem like an appropriate type of person for me and that I did not know what I wanted. Furthermore, just because he was older that did not necessarily mean he was more mature. He had many more habits unfavorable for a couple's relationship. I was naïve and did not see what my mother's experience saw. He did not have any goals for his future and wandered from city to city. Mother recognized this trait, having lived through the same experience with father. On the other hand, because I had always been with my family and valued the relationships, I wanted to establish a home of my own.

Like most women, I believed I could change his behavior and that with time he would stay put in a single place to raise our beautiful family. Every time we argued, my boyfriend yelled he was not born to be tied down to a home. My mother's words frequently came to mind and I asked myself, why I hadn't trusted mother's wisdom? At that point, I felt it was late to correct my mistake.

Despite the differences and difficulties, there were moments when we would reach agreements as we strived to make the relationship work. I thought the most important aspect was to survive, so we planned to have a child. Perhaps we thought that a baby would be the element that could unify us. Naively, I believed that a son would change my boyfriend's instability and he would have a greater reason than me to motivate his change.

Thus, not long afterwards I became pregnant. However, seven months into the pregnancy the unexpected occurred. Returning home from a weekend party, the police pulled my boyfriend over and took him to jail because he was driving under the influence. After spending a few months in a California jail he was transferred to Colorado where he had to serve a pending sentence. When this happened, I felt as if the whole world was caving in on me.

I still had two months to go for my son's delivery and felt as if I was living a nightmare. I had not heard any news regarding father, and mother had returned to Mexico a few months earlier. I couldn't go back to living with my uncles because their house was now occupied by other relatives and there was no room for me, much less a newborn. Because I could no longer afford our apartment, I had to face the sad reality of leaving.

Once again, I had to adapt and find the courage to survive. The only worthwhile aspect of this scenario of anguish, loneliness and confusion was the beautiful relationship I had with my boyfriend's four sisters. Idalia and I got along quite well. She lived with one of her married sisters and offered to share her room with me. Not having any other option, I accepted. We both worked at the same place and could carpool together. During those difficult times, she took care of me like a guardian angel sent by God. The owners of the factory where we worked had a special affection for me and when they found out my boyfriend was in jail, they offered me their full moral support. They even organized a baby shower with all of the employees, to gift me the items my baby would need.

The desired day arrived and my son was born. I named him Milton. I had waited in anticipation for him with so much love that the feeling helped diminish the impact of having his father in jail, as well as mother and my immediate family far away. Nonetheless, I felt confused over the decisions that had driven me to those circumstances. The day Milton was born, only Idalia and I were at the hospital. We had no vehicle, so we walked to the hospital early in the morning, when I began to have labor pains. All of the people we knew were sleeping and public transportation had not yet begun running. She gave me the necessary encouragement and love I needed and did not leave me alone for a single moment. Though my delivery was emotionally difficult, I was in good health and labor went smoothly. Seeing my son for the first time mitigated my pain and I fell in love with his beautiful black eyes. Now I had a greater reason to continue striving. I wanted to offer him a beautiful future and I no longer cared if I had to sacrifice, as long as he was happy.

Maria, my boyfriend's sister, as well as all his other sisters were beautiful people and very kind to me. When the hospital dismissed me, she took us to where I lived with Idalia and Elsa, the other sister. Idalia had decorated the room and it was ready for our arrival. The first night I could not sleep because I could not stop contemplating and hugging my baby. He and I were alone and I promised him I would endeavor to provide for his wellbeing. His tenderness and vulnerability awoke something within me that I had not known before. It was the maternal instinct, which instantaneously expanded my mind and enabled my priorities to change. What an interesting phenomenon. I would have never imagined how a defenseless being that I didn't even know could turn my thoughts and emotions upside down. Before, I had struggled for mother and my siblings. Now, this little one, this newborn from my own flesh who totally depended on my care, propelled me to get up from the emotional blow I had received and to set new goals.

I was conscious that the wrong choices I had made had caused suffering not just for me, but also for those who loved me most. Now, there was no reason in the world I would allow this beautiful baby –who in spite of it all was a gift from God –to suffer. I focused my time and attention on enjoying my son every moment I could. I had the support of my boyfriend's family and occasionally our uncles would come to visit. My boyfriend was still in jail; however, he had been relocated to Colorado. When our son was one month old, my boyfriend received permission to visit him for the first time. He remained with us for one month and then had to return to the penitentiary to finish his sentence until he was eligible for parole. After he was released, we remained in California three more months and then moved to Colorado.

Once there, his brother's family offered us their support. I followed, holding on to the hope that now everything would be different. After what had happened, surely he would commit to giving Milton a home. My priority was our son's happiness and I accepted his proposal to get back together. I did not want our son to suffer his absence like I had to do with my father when I was small. I would remember what I had lived: abandonment, rejection in school, loneliness and I was terrified thinking my son would have to face the cruel treatment given by children who grow up without both of their parents.

My boyfriend also had the best intention of being a good father. When he shared time with his son, he enjoyed it. To a degree, things had improved; however, once again he had problems with the police for drunk driving. This time, he caused an accident while on probation. Fearful and knowing that if he was caught again, he would have to spend several years in jail, he decided to flee the state. This time we would leave for Michigan with his cousins.

Our son was now nine months old and I was working at a nursery where I could take care of Milton while working at the same time. This was a wonderful advantage. I had made new friendships and we were adapting to the new place. I could not stand the idea of having to leave everything again; nonetheless, for our son I would do whatever I had to do. My son's father would leave to find a job and then send for us later.

One month later, I packed our clothes –yet another time– which was the only thing I could take. I boarded a plane with my little one and headed toward a new destination. Maria, my sister-in-law, called a few days later advising me to stay in Colorado so I would not lose the job I had, where I was also learning English quickly because I was working only with English speakers. In Michigan, I would have to start all over again and what was worse, I'd have to do it far away from my family. Furthermore, Maria considered it important for my boyfriend to learn to face the consequences of his actions and stop fleeing from his problems. Still, I ignored her words and once again went to live with him.

Rolling from one place to the other

I arrived in Michigan in May of 1997. It was a cold day and the only familiar faces were my boyfriend's and my son's. I now found myself further away from my siblings and mother and from my boyfriend's sisters, whom I regarded and loved like my blood relatives. My mind was a whirlwind full of dreams, which faded with each decision and new turn in life. My son's father had arrived to live with his cousin, Ana, her husband and two-year old son who were very kind and welcomed us with joy. Ana was a friendly and hardworking woman. She was pregnant and expecting a girl. We remained with them for a few months with the hope, once again, that everything would be better and that our lives would finally change. In fact, they did change but not as I expected. The difficulties between us continued and I began to realize that perhaps we should not stay together. Nevertheless, I continued clinging to illusions of a change that never came.

In spite of all the efforts made on behalf of both of us, the experience of time served in jail, his family's advice, my pleas, our beautiful son, the instability of having to flee and change residence again… none of these experiences shook my boyfriend sufficiently to generate a definite change. Our relationship once again faltered, because my son's father persisted in living the same lifestyle he always had, going to parties and getting drunk into the late hours of the night. He was used to his routine and could not see beyond that moment. He did not think about the future, the consequences for his health, he did not consider the implications in our relationship or analyze the example he was setting for his son. He did not fear the law or jail. This behavior is clearly what yuo call being unteachable. He had not learned from his experiences and he did not want to change.

This is when many women and families make erroneous and grave mistakes. We observe a son, brother, friend or spouse in similar conditions after we have given them many opportunities. Yet we persist, and stay beside them often out of fear, only to end up becoming facilitators of their destructive conduct. Yes, you and I are greatly responsible that these people don't change! We believe they will change as a consequence of our putting up with their behavior, when what really occurs is we are diminishing their opportunities for change. A person in these conditions should be allowed to fall until they reach rock bottom. One cannot continue rescuing, giving, providing money, housing and allowing them to make a disaster not only of their life, but also of our life and of the lives of others involved. Frequently, this is what psychologists call enablers; people who facilitate negative conducts. Therefore, we would be wise to break up these sponsoring structures, because what they do is very harmful. right. We need to wake up first! While we definitely need to extend forgiveness, they must still learn to face the consequences resulting from their decisions. Sadly, pain, firmness, dealings with the law and controlling ourselves from not rescuing people who don't want to learn are the best decisions and actions we can make help these loved ones.

On the other hand, I wanted another life for my son and me. My desire to better myself did not allow me to continue remaining with my boyfriend. So, I sought work and saved enough money to buy my first car. A friend taught me how to drive. I passed the exam and this helped me to no longer have to depend on others or wait for their initiatives and decisions. I acquired a valuable degree of independence when I was able to mobilize myself and had economic resources available. The first step for a person who may be tied down by someone who does not want to assume responsibility is to find economic independence. In this country, it means finding work and transportation to get there, wherever that may be. My suggestion is do not remain in these circumstances waiting for a change to occur! Ask God, take action and the path will open up for better things than you can imagine.

I felt lonely in Michigan and had no support from a nearby relative. Since I could not count on my son's father, who lived in his own world, the people that I counted on were friends from work. A few years went by and our relationship continued to deteriorate while I persisted blindly and obstinately making the effort so that my son would not live without his father. The weekend fights had become customary and if that was not enough, we had reached the point of pushing, insulting, using frequent sarcasm and disrespecting each other.

When analyzing my son's father, although he was a good man he had a difficult childhood. His father was killed in El Salvador during his adolescence. One of his bothers, with whom he had a good relationship, had also died in a car accident around the same time. He had grown up with his sisters and friends. I tried to understand his behavior and didn't know how to provide greater support. No matter how much I spoke with him, directing him to choose a more peaceful way of living, he chose not to listen.

No doubt, each of us had good intentions and desired for the relationship to function, but we found no way to make it work. We did not have guides or counselors. We were surrounded by people who lived in the same manner or worse, than we did. I spoke often with mother, in Mexico and then in Florida, yet I did not tell her anything of what I was experiencing. I did not want her to worry and possibly get sick. Besides, I felt guilty of my own situation and never forgot her words of warning. During these years, I only communicated with my siblings by phone and mail. The only people that gave us advice were my boyfriend's cousins; however, he did not heed it. My boyfriend believed women were weak and didn't know anything. He demonstrated his chauvinism through his actions and words, disqualifying, degrading, and ignoring whatever women said concerning his hurtful conduct. He had not had the example or the authority of an emotionally healthy and mature man to guide him. Now it was a little too late for him to learn.

We also had the support of our mothers. First, his mother came to live with us to take care of our son. When she left, my mother came. They were witnesses of our quarrels and although they gave us advice, I did not see a clear way out of our situation. We had deeply hurt each other in word and deed. I thought we lived that way because we were still young, but I did not understand why we were not breaking the vicious cycle. Amidst our differences, we had purchased a house together, which I had abandoned on several occasions. Nonetheless, I kept coming back because Milton asked for his father and I could not stand to see him suffer. Time and time again, I concluded that I had to exercise even more patience with his father.

Our fights became more and more violent. This was especially true when he got drunk. His actions scared me and a few times I had to escape in the middle of the night during all types of weather, including snowstorms. He pounded the bedroom door to come in and fight with me. I would take Milton out through the window and flee, so he would not have to see the angry tantrums his father had. I would leave in the car with my son and drive around the city waiting for the lights in the house to go out, so I could safely come home. There were times we slept in the car entire nights, for fear of returning home. The next day, I would get the well-known one thousand and one apologies for his behavior the night before. His promises affirming it would never happen again evaporated with the same speed as his desire to return to the bottle to flood his thoughts, fears, insecurities and emotions.

Reflection

What aspects of yourself do you value, and which ones do you not? Why? What talents and qualities do you have? How can you develop areas that are weak today? Remember, no one is born wise. It is necessary to take time to discover and learn whom you are. Find out what your talents are and develop the ones you don't have, or want to improve. This is something that corresponds to you, since no one can do it for you.

9

HOWEVER YOU WANT TO DISGUISE IT, IT IS STILL ABUSE!

During years, I lived a relationship of abuse not realizing that I was part of the problem for not putting an end to the situation.

Today, in hindsight I realize it took me too much time to analyze, recognize what I experiencing and decide to change. I should have come out of this situation much sooner without it affecting my son and me as much as it did. For years, I lived a relationship of abuse, not realizing that I was part of the problem for not putting an end to the situation. First, I want to clarify what abuse is because many women live with it on a daily basis without even knowing it. I am not a psychologist, yet I am narrating my experience in order to offer alternatives to the many victims –that like me– continue to think these behaviors are normal and spend their entire lives putting up with them, not knowing what to do. Psychological or emotional abuse involves any physical, verbal, or non-verbal pattern of behavior that negatively interferes with the well-being and development of one or several people. It affects victims by bashing their self-esteem and distorting their self-concept. It consist of verbal abuse, (involving insults, screaming, and giving orders without considering the other person) to absurd punishments that may include denying the victim food, the capacity to leave a location or similar freedom restriction actions. From there, these behaviors can escalate to greater physical abuse including face-slapping, pushing, hitting and beatings which can result in serious injuries and even the death of one or more people.

Physical, psychological and emotional abuse occurs not only in relationships between couples, people living together, or those who are married, but also between bosses and employees, parents and children, elderly people, those who are handicapped or have some impediment which makes them vulnerable or any situation where there is a power type of relationship. We can identify if there is abuse or not when one of the two people in the relationship frequently ignores the feelings of the other. or ridicules them for their beliefs, physical appearance, age, or handicaps; it also includes insults due to the person's race, family, ideals, social and economic class or language.

The behavior and words of the abuser against their victim demean and devalue that person, allegedly because they don't know enough, or for not doing what they want. The abuser believes they have the right to constantly offend and humiliate the other person in private or in public. Abuse can take on many forms. Some people use manipulation by not allowing their victim to work. They control the money, make most of the decisions and frequently threaten to abandon the victim or demand that they leave. Others say that if they leave them, they will take their own life or the life of the one threatening to leave. They manipulate the victim with lies and constant contradictions.

These people use bodily postures and facial expressions to intimidate. In extreme cases, they use weapons to maintain an atmosphere of terror. They accuse the person of infidelity and use any other situation to insult, demean, assault and relegate their victims. They verbally abuse those who can least defend themselves such as children, women, the elderly, the depressed, abandoned, withdrawn, those filled with fear and those who believe they are not worthy or capable. Victims of abuse are not allowed to express their thoughts and frequently they are made them dependent on the abuser.

According to experts, many motives can cause a person to become an abuser. One of these reasons originates both in the abusers as well as the victim's childhood. Some people repeat the pattern they experienced while growing up in their families. Others, feeling irritated or impotent with a situation, or with themselves, channel their frustration against someone close or with less power. Although childhood plays a significant role in these destructive behaviors, it is not the only reason some become victimizers. Social and cultural patterns also influence what a person learns, including the chauvinistic roles and traditions that people experience in many countries, where women are still perceived as an inferior being that is useful only for conceiving, and they are treated simply like a piece of property.

When there is physical or sexual abuse, then undoubtedly there is emotional abuse. However, verbal abuse does not always imply there is physical abuse. When a person is a victim of physical or psychological abuse during a prolonged time, it is difficult for them to recognize they are being abused.

In general, abuse begins with small manifestations that slowly increase. If one is not sure they are being abused, they can speak with a counselor in a health center, a church or a person they trust that has experience. The best resource would be to attend the psychological services that are available in most cities. These facilitators can guide and provide support to those who want to break away from the patterns of a life of torment. For people of lower incomes suffering from domestic violence, there are also legal and social services available.

If you are undergoing a similar situation, it is likely you believe that you depend exclusively on your victimizer. This may cause you fear making it difficult to trust other people. Remember that you have the right to a life free of fear. Find someone to guide you and think about the positive aspects that life offers. Do not live as a slave! A good friend will give you strength to decide and break off your relationships with the abuser. No matter what type of character or defects you may have, no one deserves to be mistreated. Another element to consider is that if you have children, your children are receiving the horrendous consequences of your lack of action. Do not believe for a single minute that you are doing them a favor. Ask yourself, what would you advice a friend who is going through a similar situation? Do you really think it is better to bear the pain and suffer in silence? Why do you agree or disagree?

If you feel as if your hands are tied because you are financially dependent on your abuser, start by finding a job even if it is a part-time. Besides, it is important for you to open a bank account where you can save money and be prepared in case the abuse becomes more intense. You may have to leave the place you are living in without warning. Always have the phone numbers of friends available in case you need to suddenly escape. If you second guess yourself, ask other people, government institutions or religious organizations that are readily available for help and support.

You can clearly identify a few signs of dangerous or unhealthy abusive behavior . One is if you are afraid of that person, have to ask them permission to do most anything, or you must ask for money to buy basic necessities. Other examples include begging to take classes that are important for your development or having to ask to be able to go out with friends to wholesome reunions. When there is excessive control in your life and you have lost confidence in your abilities, when you feel depressed, trapped and impotent, these are also signals of abuse. Frequently, abused children tend to be isolated and aggressive. Some have nightmares or do not do well in school. Do you observe any of these characteristics, attitudes or behaviors in yourself or in your children?

No person should have to live under the physical or psychological abuse of another being. This is an impediment to one's development and growth in different areas and generates stagnation. In addition, the victim will not be able to reach their goals because their abuser will not allow them to express his or her individuality for fear of abandonment or loss of control. As we have seen in my case, many times the victim wants to help the abuser change and improve their behavior, but reality is something else. When a person is constantly exposed to abuse, that person loses the capacity to think objectively and can no longer help efficiently. Help should come from a qualified professional, who is experienced and competent to do so.

VAWA Laws for Victims of Abuse

In order to inform people who may be living a similar type of situation, we offer a short description of the 1994 law that the United States Congress passed to protect women victims of domestic violence. The acronym of this law stands for, Violence Against Women Act, or VAWA. This law favors all abused people in America, regardless of citizenship status.

In some abuse situations, when a victim is undocumented, abusers threaten to call immigration to have them deported or scare them with the possibility that they may lose their children. They do this to ensure the victim remains fearful and will not abandon them. Nevertheless, in the United States, abandoning the home, on behalf of either of the spouses is not considered a crime and cannot be used against a person during any legal proceeding.

Is it possible for someone to obtain legal permanent residency under the VAWA law?

The short answer is yes, provided two conditions are met. Both conditions under this special immigration provision are:

1. That the person has been abused

2. That the victim had been married or recently divorced from a North American citizen, or legal permanent resident.

In certain circumstances, these victims can make a self-request petition before the law, without their abusive spouse (a) knowing about this petition or (b) having to help for them.

If you were never married with the abuser, or if your abuser is not a North American citizen or a permanent legal resident, you probably do not qualify for help under VAWA.

I and U type visas

However, there is another option for which you may qualify and these are Visas type I and U. What are these types of visas for? There is another law which is for victims of sexual trafficking, known as Victims of Trafficking and Violence Protection Act of 2000. This law establishes two new types of immigration law that protects people victimized through sexual trafficking. This crime is growing in various countries and both visas were designed to provide legal status to people who desire to cooperate with the authorities to help solve these types of crimes specifically. Visa Type U was designed for people who are not citizens who:

1. Have suffered physical or mental abuse due to this criminal activity

2. Posses information related to this crime

3. Agree to assist the government in furthering related investigations

4. Have lived these criminal situations within the United States or one of their territories

If you are living a similar situation, the best advice I can give you is for you to find an expert in immigration law and obtain guidance for your particular case. It will certainly be important for you to realize that as a victim you are not in the best position to help your abuser. Change in any person occurs only if they have accepted that they have a problem and are willing to seek the necessary help. Until this occurs, the victim will not be at peace. They will be fearful and no one around them will be at peace. Additionally, all those involved will all be exposed to getting seriously hurt or even killed. Is it really worth it to live like this?

Reflection

The worst moment to decide to live with another person is when you are not well, or you are confused, needy or sad. It is better to deal with one's own life and resolve the internal conflicts first, so as to be whole and then know what it is you seek in another person. What type of person would you like to share your life with? What goals do you share in common? What have you got to offer them?

I left home fleeing from mother, instead of staying to learn to live together. What I did was get myself into a worse situation. It is wiser to listen to the people who love us most because they often see details in our circumstances that we cannot see, and may be detrimental to us. Learn that your suffering also causes those who love you, and therefore have your best interest in mind, to suffer with you. However, ultimately, no matter how much your father and mother will suffer with you, you will suffer the deepest consequences.

1. *When you flee from yourself, you will take your problems with you. What are you fleeing from? Which of your decisions have caused you pain, destruction and serious consequences?*

2. *Are you an abuser? Are you willing to find help?*

3. *Are you a victim of abuse? In what ways? Do you need help to overcome this abuse situation? Do you know where you can find this help near your house?*

4. *Do you need support to overcome the masochism or sadism and the discouragement and depression that both can cause? If you are afraid or feel trapped, go to a church, or governmental organization where they can refer you to a professional counselor.*

5. *In any case, do not continue down the path you are going! Decide not to continue as an abuser or as a victim. Overcome this situation and learn to fly. The decision is yours.*

10

ALL OF MY STRENGTH AND COURAGE TO DECIDE

I decided that the game had to stop then and forever.

Finally, because of my personal experience and the knowledge I was acquiring from these situations, I became conscious of the responsibility I bore in allowing my son's father to continue destroying us. One day, I cried out to heaven and received the courage to make the hardest decision of my life, up to that point. I decided the game had to stop. This was only going to happen if I took the initiative to separate us from my son's father forever. I pinched myself and realized that nothing was going to change until I took the steps.

Mother and my brother Gabriel lived together in Michigan and I decided to go live with them. At that time, my son's father had been in a severe auto accident which occurred when his friend was driving drunk. This time, he nearly died and had to remain in the hospital for several months. I temporarily returned to the house with him, but with the complete understanding it was only to nurse him back to health, since his mother and family lived in California and Colorado. He had broken several ribs, a leg, an arm and had received several harsh blows to the head. His recovery was both slow as well as painful and for a long time, he could only move with the aid of a wheelchair.

Once again, with all that had occurred, my son's father's reaction was difficult to understand. He would get depressed, though family, friends and church acquaintances from the congregation I was attending would visit him. Once again, I thought that this near death experience would surely make him rethink his life and drive him to a definite change. Perhaps this time he would be inclined to reconcile with his family. However, it was not so! My boyfriend's mother came to live with us to help take care of him while I worked. Within me all hope of change died and then, with more strength I reoriented my efforts.

I dared to do the things I wanted to see in others and I did them with respect and love. I realized I did not need other people's approval to achieve my goals. I only needed to pay attention to the voice inside of me that propelled me to treat others as I wanted them to treat me; with fairness, warmth, understanding and compassion. I also learned I needed to put distance between destructive, negative, people and myself. I needed to get away from people who shattered my desires to reach a better future and sought to use others for their own interests. I became aware of how much there was available to read and learn in whatever field or topic I was interested in. Likewise, I realized I could believe what I wanted; I could expand my wings, and learn to fly.

Above all, it was important to discover I could speak with my Creator, in a place where we could always meet. There, in that place inside of my conscience, no one could interrupt my thoughts and I began to confront myself sincerely. I needed to see the negative as well as the positive within, so I could then focus on what I wanted to become. This did not depend on how I would achieve it. Initially, I needed to create a dream and later I could discover how it was going to come true. To realize there were so many possibilities filled my being with gratitude and inner happiness.

Amidst my many problems, I remembered father but I had resigned myself to the fact I would not find him. That possibility had died and now I had to focus on new dreams and thus reduce the pain that I still felt due to his absence. Besides, when I had free time, I would study English at home as well as attend school. My boyfriend had not just opposed me in studying English, he even told me I would never learn. He would discourage me so that I would not start any activity that could help me believe in myself or develop my talents and abilities. His negative words drove me to disbelieve myself.

In spite of his negativity, my inner desire to grow and become someone different motivated me. I purchased my first computer and asked a work technician to teach me how to use it. Later, I installed the Internet at home, and was up learning until the late hours of the night. I also asked my friend Mayra for help learning English. During the evenings, I would practice by speaking for one hour and she would correct me, as well as teach me new words. My goal was to prepare for a better job.

During this stage, I worked at several places, among them restaurants, a food packaging company (where the temperature was below zero all day) and a factory, assembling auto parts. I took advantage of every opportunity that presented itself, as long as it was an honest and respectable job for a woman and I gave the best of myself.

After almost one year, my son's father had recuperated. As if nothing had happened, he once again returned to his old habit of partying and drinking with his friends, while still using crutches to walk! Finally, I was convinced that he would not change. Our son, Milton, was three years old. I felt that my boyfriend no longer needed my care and as a result, I sat down to talk with him explaining that the best decision for us both was to separate. Though he did not agree, he finally accepted my firm decision. He proposed for me to stay in the house with Milton and he would go live with his friends. However, I knew that if I remained in the house he would feel entitled to enter at his every whim. I had thought of leaving him everything we had purchased together, including the house. I did not want to quarrel for anything, much less for material possessions. I trusted that with time, I could recover even more. I was interested in Milton's and my peace and security. Initially, he thought I was threatening him, so he would change and decided to give me some time to think. He then left with our son to go to California on vacation. During that time, I moved into a small apartment where I took our clothing. Though I had taken the same action so many times previously, this time I was no longer willing to continue the game of leaving and coming back. I had to start trusting that only God could strengthen me to break the pattern of years of psychological dependence.

When they returned from vacation, I picked them up at the airport and took my son's father to the house. There, my heart trembled as I said good-bye, took our son and left his side forever. He still had hopes that I would give up and return but I had lost all hope regarding our relationship. For nearly five years, I struggled to build a beautiful relationship with him and I finally realized that I was stiving to do so alone. I crashed against the sad but cruel reality that he truly did not demonstrate any intention of improving his life. I simply ran out of energy and realized that if I kept doing the same actions, I would only obtain the same results. This is the definition of insanity: to keep doing exactly the same things, while hoping that something will change. It didn't matter how much more I put into the relationship on my end, without his will and desire nothing more could be accomplished and nothing was going to change.

Likewise, many people around us follow unrealistic illusions, thinking that the longer they put up with a situation or the more they wait, they will see a definitive change. They reason, another child, more time… Nevertheless, in my case, ten years later… an almost fatal accident… drastic experiences and still nothing changed! It is necessary to place a period in the story, with a day and a time to make decisions, *changing the only one we can truly change, ourselves.*

Our departure from my boyfriend's life was not easy. He tried to stop me from leaving him in many ways. He said that no other man would ever look at me, much less having a child. He said that men would only go out with me to have fun and then abandon me. By then, I had learned quite a lot and had resolved that I would not make the same mistake of going to live with another man until we both had a strong commitment and a marriage relationship first. I would also not engage in a relationship with someone addicted to any type of vice. I had learned so much from my relationship with him and had promised myself that I would not allow another human being to drag me down. I decided that after separating from my son's father I would keep myself sexually pure until the day in which I found a man with whom I could share similar values and rebuild my life based on the marriage vow, "Until death do us part." Now I would carefully search for someone who respected and valued me, like my boyfriend had never done.

The first months after my separation were difficult, but I sought more than ever, to ask for wisdom and strength from God. I established a true relationship with my Creator and enjoyed peace as a result of my time with Him and Milton. My son's father tried to regain my heart in multiple ways, including promising me that he would go to church and come close to God. I clarified that these promises are not momentary but serious and that he should seek God because he desired to, not just to convince me to return with him. Even then, he didn't fulfill what he said.

From the time of our separation, I never prohibited our son and him from communicating. Amidst the difficulties, he was a good father and loved his son. I believed that as long as Milton's physical and emotional security were not in danger, it was important for them to develop good communication with each other. A healthy pattern of communication among separated parents includes never speaking ill about the other spouse, or challenging their decisions. Milton was aware of many situations, yet I tried to help him maintain a balanced perspective.

For a long time, at Milton's quite young, he would remember the fighting and incidents in our life. Nonetheless, with the invaluable help of friends and leaders from our church, he overcame the traumas. The most important element for me has been God's help, from whom I have derived strength to educate my son and help him overcome negative memories. Milton has also learned to love his father without fear. Now he understands his father better and prays he will be able to reconcile with his Creator and with himself. It is interesting to hear the advice that a child gives a grown man.

With time, my son's father and I have also learned to respect each other and maintain a good relationship. For our son's wellbeing and for the need that every person has of forgiving and being forgiven, I feel I have forgiven the wounds he caused us, realizing he may not have intended to inflict them. On my side, I have also asked forgiveness for my faults and deficiencies. His addiction to alcohol caused many destructive, painful and unloving situations. Likewise, I have recognized my own immaturity, my voids, rebellion and ignorance and I know I have hurt and caused him pain. I did not know how to help him come out of the hole he was in. Although I believe I did everything I could and knew how to do, I realize today that I was just as guilty as he was of several decisions we took when we started such a serious relationship as intimate cohabitation, without knowledge, appropriate tools or adequate preparation.

When mother saw that this time my separation was serious, she returned to the United States to support me. During critical moments, mother has been a fountain of inspiration, practical support, strength and courage. Feeling her love toward me has been essential for me to continue on when I felt desperate. She not only encouraged me, but also my son. For a time, all we had were each other. Our love helped us overcome obstacles and find happiness.

Mother began to work a different schedule than mine so that between the two of us, we would be able to take care of Milton. We had brought my sister Elia from Mexico and I signed her up to finish High School while she worked in the evenings. However, during that time problems with my son's father had escalated and I had to send her to my uncle's house in Ohio. Not long after that, we brought her back to live with us. Time was rolling by and although I was getting used to my new life, I was full of questions.

Reflection

Now that I am an adult I ask, why do such few people confront those who are irresponsible, those who oppress and violate the rights of other individuals? Why don't we confront those who hurt fragile people? When we come in contact with cases like these, we ought take actions to denounce them. This is even more valuable when they are our own relatives and friends!

Often, those who are oppressed are afraid, and don't know what to do. Society, and more specifically YOU and I, can help to not perpetuate injustice. We can unite and become a strong force when we act together. Are you ready to advocate for the unprotected and go a few steps beyond? What practical and realistic actions, which do not generate dependence, can you carry out?

11

UNCOVERING FAMILY AND CULTURAL WOUNDS

Culturally, we have learned to silence ourselves… The culture of silence covers up, hides, and buries our deep pain and shame.

My parents married in 1978. Initially, father was responsible and loving (like most newlyweds tend to be). However, as often occurs in many marriages, when the honeymoon is over a few months later, true personalities are revealed in broad daylight. Father returned to his former habits as if he were a single man and in his case, he had the habit of wandering off alone to dances and participating in religious festivals and parties, which are common in the Hispanic culture and Catholic faith. The problem was not these gatherings in and of themselves, but the quantity of alcohol that people are used to consuming there. Father not only drank until he lost awareness of what he was doing, he danced with whichever woman he wanted in his drunken state. Of course, mother could not do the same!

Many people have an incorrect perception of manhood. Often males try to keep women enslaved, while they unbridle all of their desires. Part of the problem is that men try to impose this law; however, the real issue is that women allow it! This is inconceivable. How can a woman, in this day and age, allow herself to be used like a mop, or a doormat? What is worse is that many women, like my mother, were taught to accept verbal and physical abuse, and unending infidelities, with all of their consequences! As if that was not enough, people use God to justify that position and to perpetuate it, instead of confronting the situation and steering both individuals and couples toward a healing process. This is like trying to cover the sun with one's finger and ignore a huge societal ill that makes many families' lives miserable! It was common for families to teach their girls that this type of treatment is an expression of love towards a woman. They would say such absurd things as, if your husband is not treating you this way it is because he does not love you.

Consequently, many women in similar cultures still believe that ill treatment means their spouse, or partner, loves them. The scourge in many societies continues because women are modeling the acceptance of this behavior in front of their boys and girls!

Father, of course, did not allow mother to ask him about their finances; how much he earned, or how he spent (wasted) their money. She could not ask for explanations about the places where he went or anything that had to do with key family decisions. When they attended the parties together, near grandmother's house, he would leave mother at grandmother's house and had the audacity to go to the party by himself. What consideration and love, right? He would drop into the house periodically, to ensure that mother was there like an animal waiting for its master. If this is not lowly treatment on behalf of men, what is it? On a certain occasion, they went to a wedding and as usual, he danced with all the girls he wanted. Mother also liked to dance; but she would have to beg him to dance with her and still he refused her entreaties. A young man whom the family knew asked mother to dance and she accepted. When father saw her, immediately his ego was under attack and he came up from behind, drove his elbow into her back, and told her to go pick up the children because it was time to go home. This was mother's enchanting life.

At that time, my parents had three children, Gabriel, who was two months old, Dioselina and me. They left the party and on the way home father was quite upset and began arguing with her. Her great sin was to have allowed another man to dance with her and touch her. When they got home, father beat her, although this time it was with a leather belt. With that abusive demonstration of anger, mother became quite saddened. She could not conceive of what father had done. His anger was inexcusable and brutal. After that, justifying his actions, father thought it very cute to return to the party and continue dancing and drinking, but alone!

A person who lives this type of situation or knows someone who does should stop and ask if in this situation, his or her culture is contributing something favorable and worthy of perpetuating for future generations. Please, it is time that older women wake up and stop condoning this abuse for themselves, or their daughters.

Well, on that occasion, father stayed out all night and came back the following morning, falling over in a state of stupefaction. He then beat mother again and proceeded to throw her out of the house. Mother left with her three little ones and went to grandma's house. However, in the evening after the effects of his vice had passed, he arrived along with his parents, begging mother to return with him. He publicly asked for forgiveness and recognized he was culpable for having been so drunk; as if his drunkard state justified the injustice. As always, he swore it would never happen again. He even cried in front of them as he gave mother accolades saying he knew he did not deserve anything from her. Of course, appealing to her conscience and noble heart, he was able to convince her to come back with him. How many more times was she to bear this? What for? Did anything change? Nothing. Absolutely, nothing!

However, she went back with him due to my grandparent's strong insistence and their affirmations that she had to assume her responsibility as a wife because she had chosen him and had children with him. Besides, she could not be floating from house to house. Thus, mother, who was used to submitting to her parents, obeyed. It is sad to see that traditionally, and perhaps due to financial reasons, this used to be, and in many cases still is, the advice given to daughters regardless of how traumatic that coexistence may be. Those counselors perpetrate a pathological system that does not resolve anything. So, as was to be expected, when mother returned with father, the situation worsened.

Father's partying engagements became more frequent and beating mother upon returning home became a habit. The next day, he would simply ask for forgiveness with the same old excuse of not being able to remember anything that had happened. He often used this excuse, yet mother did not have her family's support or another place to go with her children. Therefore, she endured years of ill treatment in silence without the right to even complain or ask for help. She eventually learned the routine that when father went out to dance, and spent time with his "lovers" (her acquaintances kept her informed), mother could not confront him, for fear she would get another whipping to silence her and deter any question or complaint. There were times when father would leave the house for days and mother would be alone with her little ones, without food or resources to buy groceries, since the town was far away. The only option she had was to make atole, a corn based drink, and tortillas; this was the food she could offer us.

Father's other facet was his instability. He did not take root anywhere. Instead he constantly immigrated to other cities in and out of the country. According to him, it was easier to find work elsewhere and it was paid better. During his absences, we would stay at grandmother's house. Little by little, father became more used to living far away from his family, without responsibilities and without having to see or pay the consequences of his actions.

When my father would finally return home, he would do so for a few months at a time and then leave again. My mother would be pregnant, once again and the game started all over with mother alone, but with another belly and greater responsibilities. When he would leave to go to the United States, mother could then save from the monies he sent, at the expense of depriving herself of basic necessities, for the times he didn't send enough funds. In this manner, she was able to save for a plot of land, with the hope that he would return and would never have to leave us again.

Instead of improving, when father left for the US, the situation got worse. The distance only served to detach him completely from physically taking care of his kids. He could no longer help to bathe, feed or take them to the doctor when they were ill or help with their homework. As the saying goes, "eyes that don't see, heart that doesn't feel," and for father there was no more urgency, because he did not see our plight or feel it in his own flesh. My grandparents continued helping mother out, as best they could. In reality, my father was a very selfish person, who only thought about his own pleasure and wellbeing and he left mother a burdensome responsibility, which was not just unfair, but too heavy a load for anyone.

However, every time that mother mentioned to my grandparents she was thinking of leaving father they would oppose her because divorce was not an option. They said that a woman married for life and she had to bear everything her husband did, including extreme poverty and endless infidelity. So, doesn't a man also marry for life and promise fidelity, like a woman does? Do you think this is a misperception which is also harmfully blinding? What a myopic interpretation to think that God sponsors such abuse and distortion of the marriage covenant. In their ignorance, even religious people use God so that women will continue in those pathological relationships, while men keep getting away with what they do. These people do not even think of looking at the commandments of God regarding sexual exclusiveness within marriage and outside of it. My, how things are distorted, wouldn't you agree?

In summary, my grandparents justified father's actions, saying that all marriages went through those stages and that someday he would change.

Mother was simply supposed to bear with it, "for her children's sake." My grandparents considered divorce to be an embarrassment and mother would not be the first woman to get a divorce in the family. According to the traditions of our towns, chauvinism and jealousy were present in every home. Father, came from a home which suffered from a similar situation and they believed the same.

Mother, on the other hand, had not seen this type of behavior. Her father was a humble, hard working person who enjoyed his home. When mother got engaged with father, my maternal grandfather advised her not to marry him. He knew how dad's family lived, yet mother did not listen and sooner, rather than later, she suffered the consequences.

What happened with my father, mother and siblings?

Shortly after arriving in the United States, I personally inquired of my uncles about the last information they had about **father's** whereabouts. They shared with me what they suspected happened and different versions of stories they had. Some people affirmed that one night, while father was driving drunk he had run over a woman and her daughter, both of whom had died. They supposed that due to this involuntary crime, he had perhaps been incarcerated and sentenced to many years in prison. However, none of his brothers, or acquaintances could confirm this rumor or the state in which it had happened.

With the information regarding the last places where father had lived and with the help of a girlfriend from work who spoke English, I sent letters and a photograph of father to the jails in those states. Some of the penitentiaries replied saying they had found no one with that information in their institution. Other jails never replied.

Then, I sent the same information and picture to a Hispanic television program that was known nationwide, with the hope they would transmit the information and someone who knew of him would respond. However, no one responded to my letter or returned father's picture. Lastly, I called the restaurants where, according to my uncles, father had last worked. They did not have any information about him either.

Another version was that he had remarried and gone to live with another woman and now had a new family. This story was also unconfirmed and no one ever saw him with another family. To this day, on the date I am writing this book, we still do not know how he died. We've had to resign to the fact that some things are mysteries and we will not know them in this life.

Mother has never again remarried. She has devoted herself solely to her children and grandchildren. Besides, after that experience with father, she really did not have much of a desire to start another relationship. Perhaps if she would have known a man with much less of a chauvinistic mentality, who would support her and see her as his equal, as a partner and not as an inferior person, her children would have supported her in establishing her life with another man. Where are those types of men? Sadly, we are lacking people of the masculine gender, who genuinely embrace the value of women, not just with sweet little words, but also with actions.

Today, amidst a wrongly named sexual revolution, the status of women is still predominantly devalued and cheapened in many parts of the world. Often times, society still views women primarily as sex symbols and agents of procreation when they have so much more to give. However, for this to occur, a young girl must be brought up to recognize her potential, so she can excel and make contributions in any field.

Since father disappeared, mother has not had a single boyfriend. It would be beautiful for her to open up to the possibility of a healthy and mature relationship during the golden years of her life. How nice it would be for her to find someone that would complement her, with whom to share joys and sorrows. No matter what, we, her seven children, will care for her and seek to give her back a little of all she has given for us.

Since I came to live in the United States, I have not been able to return to Mexico; I have not seen my sister Dioselina, (or Cheli, as we call her endearingly), nor have I met her two beautiful children, Estefania Monserrat and Alan Miguel. I have only seen them in pictures and videos. Dioselina's husband is Arturo, and I met him when he was on his way to Ohio. I really should give credit where credit is due. I greatly admire my sister because, in spite of having lived most of her life far away from mother, she has done a wonderful job of raising and caring for our younger siblings up to the age where they were able to care for themselves.

Dioselina has sincerely been a mother for all of my siblings and part of the tribute of this book is for her. My dear little sister is a go-getter, who after getting married and having children, returned to school to finish her accounting career with much sacrifice. When we speak via the telephone, she often tells me of some other goal or dream she has set for herself. For me, she is an example of determination, and has taught me that half of a battle is won when one has the desire to overcome obstacles. A person who has a clear vision will be better equiped to overcome obstacles that come along, though it may take them more time than with more resources or less restricting circumstances. What is admirable is that she continued on until she conquered her dream. Dioselina understands that excuses for not attaining our goals are many, but what is important is to find ways that will lead us ever closer to our ideals.

Cheli, I love you very much. You are an extraordinary woman! You are learning to love your family, to forgive our parent's flaws and to support mother when she has needed it. You have also raised your own family without abandoning our siblings. You have suffered difficult moments alone, with little support from mother or me. You have overcome many situations with determination and maturity. You transmit values you have practically learned on your own to your children, taking personal initiative to give what is good and isolating yourself from what is not profitable. Now, you are dedicated to helping your children fulfill their goals. They have not had to suffer the void of a broken home or the absence of their parents. You have wisely determined to grow your marriage, amidst a modern society that has not learned what respect or family values are. Continue transmitting your values and love of life to your children and to the world, and in that regards, never change.

To my brother Gabriel and Israel, the two males of the family –who have worked in the US for a while– but currently reside in Mexico. I am very proud of you. Both of them are married. Gabriel's daughter is Leslie and Israel's is Alaina. As I write this book, Israel's second daughter was born, and they named her Alison. Both of my brothers are good fathers, and responsible men who strive to better circumstances for their family. They are examples of how we can transform serious obstacles into blessings.

Gabriel, when you were only eight years old, you assumed the role of a man. I remember you preferred to continue wearing your torn pants but we never lacked our daily bread and milk at home. I thank God for the courage he gave you to endure our many difficulties. I admire and appreciate your strength to take care of us. You assumed the role of father in our family and defended us from people's cruelty. When I was living a hell of solitude during my adolescence, you made me feel protected, loved and admired. You have gotten up repeatedly from many falls and though you could have made decisions that would have ruined the rest of your life, you decided not to do so. This takes courage and strength. Your character has allowed you not to become another youth statistic of adolescents who have grown without a paternal figure and ended up doing drugs, alcohol, gangs and delinquency. When I think about you, I see a loving man who is a hard worker, courageous and a dreamer. I know that the best is yet to come to your life.

Israel, you tender hearted brother of mine. I remember you with that sad look, which you inherited from father. You were always willing to carry out any task we needed. Although you were quite young when you began working, I never heard you complain or reject any employment offer no matter how rough it was. You have taken up new challenges with courage and a noble spirit. I appreciate the love and respect with which you have treated mother, in spite of the fact that you spent the majority of your life far away from her. Today, you are an excellent father and husband. Your character provides stability to the family as well as to mother; I am proud of you. You are quiet; nevertheless, your actions demonstrate how much you love your family. As a youngster, you renounced your education in order to work, recognizing the financial burden we had and thus helping to carry everyone's weight. During the difficult adolescent years, you also resisted temptations to follow illusions and harmful paths. When I have sat down to make suggestions concerning your life, you have accepted my words and applied them. You are not characterized by the pride that defines so many men and makes them deaf. I value your obedience and love for your family. I am proud of your achievements as a father, husband and son.

Elia, you were always the most introverted, from when you were little. You don't express your emotions much, but you receive our love. When mother had to leave, you sought refuge, warmth, shelter and the love of a mother in your older sister, me; I was your world. I remember your words of admiration, and how you defended me adamantly. However, like mother, I too disappointed and abandoned you although I didn't want to. When mother left, you did not understand what was happening, but when I left, it was a second blow, a harsh one for you because you were a little older then. You begged me not to leave you, but I wanted to give you so many material things that I ignored your pleas. You were in good hands with Cheli; however, this was not what you needed, or wanted. You wanted your mother and older sister to be near you! Of all of us, the one who has suffered emotionally the most of all in this story is you! Forgive us for having hurt you so deeply, though we did not desire to do so.

Years later, Elia emigrated and came to live with me. She was only an adolescent and the plan was that she could work and go to school. However, her story took another course; one full of challenges and tragedy. Truly, the one who most reaped the consequences of our triple desertion was Elia. First it was father, next, to support the family, mother left and thought it pains me to recognize it, I too physically abandoned my siblings. Eventually, she came to live with me in Michigan. A while back we had met a cousin on my father's side who managed a Mexican restaurant in Ohio. We trusted him because he was our uncle. I was going through my separation, precisely at that point, when we visited this uncle and told him about Elia. Very kindly, he offered help by giving Elia a job.

Believing in his good intentions, we had no concerns over accepting his help. We thought it would be a good opportunity for Elia to start earning money to support herself. She was only sixteen years old and looked as if she was ready to take on this new challenge. I could not offer her much support in the midst of my own unstable situation. Therefore, I left her near her new work place and returned to Michigan, trusting she was in good hands. As the months passed, Elia started to change. We noticed she sounded somewhat strange on the phone. Nevertheless, when we visited her, everything seemed normal. Then mother went to live with her and confirmed that something was wrong. Elia was always arriving late at night, supposedly because she was working. She spent lots of time sleeping and was always feeling tired. Mother would ask what was going on, but she evaded her questions.

At no point did mother think that our uncle had anything to do with her daughter's strange behavior. She was clueless and even mentioned the situation several times to him, requesting him to speak with her, to know what was going on and thus be able to help her. Kindly, he agreed to help her... the evil hypocrite! The weeks and months rolled by, but the maternal instinct warned mother that something serious was occurring. Then mother and Elia came to Michigan to visit us. The idea was to get Elia out of her environment to be able to speak with her openly. This was when Elia confessed she was pregnant. She made up a story of her child's father, which made no sense. Mother had never seen her go out with any boy. The only man with whom her daughter spent time was with our uncle; but with such willingness to help and the appearance of goodness he had, mother denied accepting he would have been directly involved with my sister's pregnancy. Nonetheless, there was no one else on the scene; absolutely no one else spent time with Elia.

Of course, Elia denied that uncle was the father or her baby and mother did not have the courage to ask him directly. Our uncle was married and had children. Not only was it something shameful for mother to ask this type of question, but she was afraid of our uncle's family, because they could hurt my sister. Therefore, mother decided to keep silent and support her daughter during the rest of her pregnancy.

Culturally, we have learned to remain silent. It is a culture of silence, which covers up, hides, and buries issues. Our silence holds deep pain and shame. What is worse is we all know that what is happening is a terrible evil. Besides, our silence does not allow for justice to roll down. Keeping silent makes us accomplices of evil, including the evil that runs through our own families; evils like incest, beatings, ill treatment, lies, children born and repudiated for not having a surname –stealing and treason, among other horrendous social ailments.

The human condition brings shame to us and we prefer to keep suffering than to open up the rotten pot; to confront and put an end to the lies and hypocrisy. This is how evil people appear to be so good before society. They commit crimes that remain unpunished, though they may be killing the souls of the innocent. These deaths go undeclared and are never heard before a tribune or jury, though their victims suffer for a lifetime. People perpetuate the culture for fear of retaliation. However, today is another era. Humanity has evolved, in general and at least in some parts of the world. There are laws of protection; though justice may not always be accomplished when destructive behaviors are uncovered. It is time to speak out, to unmask and to confront those who hurt others; especially the defenseless. No matter what the family ties may be, what the social position is or the fortunes that stand behind a person, it is time to denounce this behavior. Stop covering up this wickedness! Mother should have spoken out, but she was overpowered by fear.

When Elia was about seven months pregnant, another of these unpunished crimes occurred. It was then that mother confirmed that our uncle was the father of Elia's child. She ended up at the hospital and almost lost the baby.

It was vengeance; she received a terrible beating on behalf of the members of our uncle's family. This unjust situation increased mother's suffering. The one they should have beaten –besides throwing him in jail– was our uncle. He was over thirty years of age, and gotten a sixteen-year-old pregnant –a farm girl who trusted her uncle. To make matters worse, Elia was not out of danger. Our uncle's wife was so blinded that instead of taking out her anger on her adulterous husband, she took it out on an inexperienced and naïve girl. She arranged the beating in an attempt to kill the young girl and the child fathered by her husband. Our uncle entered our lives as a rapacious wolf who posed as a lamb, dressed in compassion, and doing Good Samaritan deeds. Later he took advantage of the immaturity of a young, insecure girl, who lacked love.

His crime was a triple one. First, he deceived and seduced her. Then he covered himself with a blanket of shame and exposed the lives of both Elia and his unborn child with lies, blaming her before his family. As if these actions were not enough, he deserted her. His abandonment was financial and emotional, not just physical. Elia, once again experienced yet another rejection. Our uncle did not even have the courage to defend her before his wife, accepting his culpability. When the child was born, of course mother was there once again, supporting her daughter. Our uncle did not show up to assume his paternity; the coward hid behind his wife's skirt, washed his hands, and evaded the family.

How many actions like these plague the earth, day after day? In every country, society allows men, propelled by their uncontrolled animal instincts to dishonor girls and produce innocent offspring who did not ask to come into this world. Thus, the custom is perpetuated because there is not enough social pressure to punish this evil with strong consequences that would reduce the infamous crime to a minimum. What's more, society considers it something normal. It is time to denounce; it is time to identify those who commit these acts, and it is time to take united action. Our uncle escaped earthly justice; however, everything one sows eventually they will reap. There is a Just Administrator, who does not overlook even the foolish words we speak, much less our actions. We do not wish vengeance for our uncle, but genuine repentance both before God, Elia and his son, so he may have internal peace, and to some degree, to bring relief to those who had to live with the consequences of his actions. What would be best, however, is to go a step further. That step is called RESTITUTION! Our uncle and anyone that hurts a person, should compensate for their damage in some form that is accepted by the victim(s). This truly, would be revolutionary at the judicial level and is exactly what divine justice teaches.

Time lapsed and apparently, Elia overcame this horrible stage, along with her son. However, the truth is that she continued a life of abuse, which escalated time after time and stiffled her. Later, she met another young man which mother did not consider was a good fit. This man also liked to get drunk. Anyone could ask, what is wrong with alcohol consumption? In moderation, one or two glasses are not a problem. The essence of the problem is that people don't know how to control themselves, they can't just drink a little but they go overboard and lose control of themselves, of their thoughts and their actions.

For a person with this habit, nothing good can await them along the road. Elia did not listen to mother's wise counsel and there she went again. History repeats itself; Elia went to live with that man. A few months later, Elia finally opened up and told us that he abused her too.

My brothers intervened on several occasions, but Elia kept returning when he promised he would not beat her again. The cycle never improved and mother got tired of giving her advice concerning her pathological relationship. Many women barely realize they are responsible for their abusive situations. Perhaps, someone is not responsible for the first time this type of situation happens, but to "trip again, with the same rock," as the popular song goes, is one's own fault for remaining in a relationship knowing the consequences. Elia continued that path and had her second and third child with that man. Not much later, Elia called us. She was in trouble. Her boyfriend was in jail; they had fought and he had again abused her. This time, she had called the police and the situation had quite an unexpected shift.

Due to her boyfriend's illegal status and his abuse toward her, he was deported. Elia was now alone with three children, and the youngest was a newborn. With all that had happened, when mother visited her we observed symptoms of a deep depression. My sister was not only very nervous, but she had turned violent with her children. Mother thought it was due to the frustration of having to raise them on her own. Elia said no one understood her and that she felt like she was struggling and working just to survive, pay bills and her children's nursery. Though she tried, she would blow her temper and frequently lose control in her dealings with her little ones.

One day, we received a phone call from the police informing us they had arrested Elia the previous night; the three minors were in a temporary home. They accused her of negligence in the care of her children and of being a threat to their lives. Elia had lost control and severely abused her eldest son. She had also threatened the children while the neighbors were listening, which was the reason why they called the police. Elia also told the officers that she needed urgent help. That night, they took her to jail, because the police was not aware of her mental state. During the time she remained in jail, other people further abused Elia both mentally and physically. Her condition, no doubt, worsened!

When we tried to assume legal custody of her three children, it was too late. They were under State custody and it would not be easy for them to us award us their custody unless we qualified in different areas. Mother could not even visit Elia for fear that immigration would deport her. On top of it all, she did not want to end up deported. Our only communication with Elia was a brief daily telephone call. However, due to her illegal status in the country, Immigration took over Elia's case, and no attorney wanted to defend her. A person in these circumstances did not have much of a chance to win. Now, she was on the verge of deportation and could lose the option of recuperating her children definitely.

Elia's world tumbled down! She felt trapped and with no way out. Her hope was slowly dying, day by day. Mother and I began to anchor our faith in a real and living God, who intervenes and transforms our dark realities, when we invite him to do so. We took up God's promises and requested His guidance in favor of Elia's case. To the surprise of all, the judge miraculously changed the verdict and allowed Elia out of jail on conditional bail. Later, a psychiatric hospital admitted her. Though it was a nightmare, especially for mother, it was better for her to be in a hospital in the U.S. than for immigration to have deported her, where we would not have seen her again.

The story did not take a turn here. When Elia left the hospital, after receiving mental and emotional treatment, she once again allowed another man to get close, engaging in yet another romantic relationship. This individual took advantage of her frail and vulnerable condition, while she was still under the effects of medication. As commonly occurs in the egotistical satisfaction of desires, where there is no commitment, or love, thought or reflection and much less the consideration of possible implications, this man also got her pregnant, only to abandon her one more time! Elia, obviously destroyed emotionally, continued spiraling downward, which led to her almost losing custody of her fourth and last child. At this time Alma, our other sister and William, her husband, were able to adopt him.

Today, Elia remains under permanent medical care, in and out of the hospital, where she receives medications that control her mental condition. With the birth of her third child, she experienced a deep post partum depression and she did not seek help in the medical profession nor in her family, but ignored it thinking it would soon go away. However, her mental state worsened and doctors diagnosed her with psychosis and schizophrenia.

These disorders turned her aggressive and she is dangerous to the people she lives with. The mental condition causes her to hear voices that order her to hurt and manipulate people to obtain what she wants. Elia's oldest son is under the temporary custody of his father; yes, our famous uncle. Surprisingly, the child's father and his wife have favorably reconsidered their actions and accepted their responsibility. The boy is now growing up with his step siblings and developing well. We are in permanent and direct contact with him through the social worker assigned to his case, who keeps us informed. He participates in sports activities along with the other children the couple has.

Elia's two other children are on the verge of adoption by a family who has been caring for them. Although their father returned to the United States from Mexico and wants to gain custody of his children legally, he has not been able to do so because of his illegal status and physical abuse charges against my sister. My husband and I have appealed for the children's custody; however, because we live in another state, the courts have not yet granted a final verdict concerning moving the children. What is most important for our family is that the children are safe, loved and well taken care of, wherever foster care assigns them. We miss them and trust God will keep watch over them as well as provide all that is good.

Elia, you do not know how much mother and I would have liked to avoid all this pain in your life! We never imagined our instability would have such repercussions or that it would have affected you to that extent. Elia, we ask for your forgiveness for our failures, abandonment, neglect and for leaving you alone and unprotected, without being aware of it. Though we had no ill intent, we were naive and did not take precautions. We did not look out for you as we should have; we are deeply sorry. How could we have let a sixteen-year-old girl, live far from us with a stranger, even if he was a relative? Today, so many years later, I still don't understand. Sometimes we feel that money is too important, and we risk our own integrity without measuring the consequences.

Elia, we need to be frank with ourselves and realize that we make many mistakes for not consulting God or considering what He teaches. Often, we ignore his laws which are clearly laws of protection. Our pride is also a huge cause of pain. We do not like to hear we are doing something wrong, though we are the first ones who will suffer when consequences turn negative.

Nevertheless, there is no place too deep or too dark from where God cannot rescue you. Your story is not over yet, and God continues working within you and in your children. Put your faith in the Almighty, dialogue with Him and trust that He can work miraculously. You will always have the support of all of your siblings, mother's and your children's. We will not leave you or them alone. We love you very much. Though you have many challenges to overcome, what is most important is that you can count on our love. Never let hope die.

Elenita, my smiling girl, you are contagious wherever you go, with your beautiful smile and enthusiasm for life. You inspire me with your strength to confront challenges and the maturity with which to take advice. In spite of many difficulties in your adolescence, you have never surrendered. No one can stop you and this makes you dangerous to insecure people.

Elena finished her primary education and we arranged for her to immigrate so she could live near mother. The plan was for her to finish High School in the morning, and work in the afternoon. That way she could help contribute with the expenses where she and mother were living.

During that time, mother worked seven days a week in two different places and Elena would arrive home to an empty apartment. As could be expected, shortly after coming to the U.S. she started a relationship with a young man who was a friend of my brothers'. When mother and my brothers became aware of it, they opposed the relationship; she was too young to have a boyfriend.

We had so many dreams for her and we knew education was a key factor. For this reason, we did not want her to be negligent with her education. In spite of our opposition, Elena continued with that relationship and a short while later, she became pregnant, dropped out of school and left to live with her boyfriend. This was another strong blow for the family, but especially for mother. History was again repeating itself.

After a few years of living with her boyfriend, she decided to leave him because she too was a victim of physical and mental abuse! For a while, she and her son lived with us, until she started to work and found her own apartment. During her free time, Elena continued her education to offer her boy a better future.

Elena, continue discovering and fulfilling the purpose that God has for you and your beautiful son, Kevin. I love you; you are the joy of our family.

Alma, you are literally the soul of our family! If I think I am strong and have a tough, fighting spirit, you surpass me. Our baby, as we call you because you are the youngest, you have demonstrated that with your high self-esteem and personal security no one can defeat you.

Alma immigrated to the U.S. a few months after Elena. She came with the same dream of studying and we signed her up at the same school with the same routine of studying in the morning and working in the evening. The reader can now imagine what happened. Yes, she met a young man, they started going steady and though we explained it was not the time for a serious boyfriend, she did not listen. Our dreams for Alma were also big. Alma enjoyed studying much more than Elena. She was ambitious and was always looking to create new projects. We knew she had the capacity to finish any career she chose. Our plan was thwarted when she too became pregnant. At this point, as a family we felt as if a chain was pulling and sinking us down, persecuting us with the same destiny. This was one month after we found out about Elena's pregnancy! She was only sixteen.

Alma, however, faced the situation in quite a different way and with maturity and determination, as did her boyfriend. They went to live with his parents and she decided to continue studying while the baby was born. Today, she is happily married to a man that turned out to be a good, responsible person who is devoted to his family. Alma has continued preparing and following her dreams to own a business. She knew her son would require time and attention until he grew up; then she could continue her education. She never viewed him as an impediment, but as an inspiration to continue receiving training.

If you want Alma to do something, tell her she cannot achieve it and you will see how fast she will finish the task. The beautiful thing is that she uses these positive traits to build a better world. I call Alma the special warrior; there is no spiritual battle that can hold her back. On the contrary, she faces each situation with courage, wisdom, strength and above all faith. Alma emits energy to those of us that surround her. I love you little sister.

We have taken so many turns and twists individually and as a family, with so many blows in the process! In the midst of it all, it is an honor for me to have been born in this home. In a family where our mother did not allow any obstacle to come between her and her seven children to teach them all she could, though she was alone. She taught us to be responsible and disciplined. She has loved us unconditionally and sacrificed her personal well-being for ours at all times. Mother, you are a heroine, the woman whom these seven children honor. You have influenced our lives for good and this is the best inheritance you could have given us. We hope to pass it on to each of our children, since the values you have transmitted are like diamonds, difficult to find. You have always been a woman of faith who believed in and loved God.

However, when Elia fell into depression and lost her children, mother was deeply saddened. We feared she could suffer a heart attack because her health was frail. Six hours away from where she lived, I could not comfort her as I would have liked to. Thus, I frequently kept her up to date concerning Elia's condition and case, based on the lawyer's information and what the jail personnel told me. This was when mother surrendered completely to God. We saw how He performed miraculously on several occasions, especially in Elia's case. Ultimately, mother realized that God was all she needed to overcome every situation, difficulty and struggle. Her priorities changed and God became not only the one she sought when she had problems, but He became number one in her life. Mother realized that to believe in God was not enough. God wants us to fully surrender to Him, to learn to seek Him and to follow His teachings. Mother would not have been able to resist the many situations that have come to her life had it not been for the strength that our Heavenly Father has given her. She has learned that He opens doors that no man can close, and closes doors that no man can open.

Mother, I implore heaven to keep you here with us for many more years to come so we can enjoy your company and give you joy. Thanks a million for each of the sacrifices you have made. We value each one!

Reflection

Dear reader, you can derive your own conclusions concerning the situations that occurred in our family. You can also infer what has been happening in your own family. What do you think? What would you like to change so that your negative situations will never repeat themselves in the history of your children and their children? What will you do to ensure these changes?

12

THE ENCOUNTER WITH MY HEAVENLY FATHER

I would have never imagined where my search would take me.

All of these experiences, situations and difficulties caused me much grief, fear and anguish. I faced many difficult moments. Several of the people with whom I lived at that stage of my life were also confused, divided, and full of bitterness, hate, selfishness and the list could go on. On the other hand, other people were joyous and kind, willing to support others sincerely. However, one of the most important lessons I learned was how to understand why people live like they do. Today, I understand that the answer to that question has to do with their convictions and beliefs. What a person believes is reflected in how he or she behaves. No doubt, actions are the external manifestation that the soul reflects. Think this over and see how true it is.

My soul was empty and I felt both impotent and disappointed when I could not find my earthly father. Yet it was precisely in that process of searching, with its prolonged frustration, that I found my Heavenly Father.

I would have never imagined where my search would take me. In my Mexican culture, I grew up hearing about the existence of God. First, I thought that the Great and all-Powerful being was not in the least bit interested in me. According to my understanding, he was too busy taking care of his creation and blessing the people who did His will, carried out charitable acts or served in some church.

For me, God was a distant being whom I could not understand or touch. I believed attending church on special days was enough to appease Him and keep Him happy. It was more a matter of performing certain rituals or ceremonies because I had never heard that one could have a personal relationship with an invisible being. As I started to mature, I realized I had a huge void in my life because of the blows I received over the years. I did not know why I was in this world, but I did know I was not doing things like God wanted. I justified my actions by telling myself that I was not perfect and that it was not my fault! It was hard for me to believe that God was interested in me and much less that he loved me. If He truly loved me, I thought, He would not have allowed father to abandon us or allow people to despise me because I was poor or allow my relationship with Milton's father to fail. In essence, I felt disappointed with God.

Certainly, a simple woman like me could not possibly interest God. I asked, what could He want me for? Why am I on this earth? These and many more questions seemed irreconcilable. For many years, I sought for the answers to these and many other questions. It seemed as if the God of the universe was hiding and was indifferent towards me.

When I came to Michigan, instead of our lives or my boyfriend's improving, I found I was more and more alone, sadder and unprotected. I feared that my son would grow up in an environment alone and with little interaction with others.

I had grown up listening to my family speak about God, especially when there were emergencies, like a fireman you call on when there are fires. Although we attended church, I did not know how to personally communicate with God. In my desperation, when nothing that happened to me seemed to make sense, I prayed to God, in the solitude of night, to help me find the path that led to Him. I realized I had much to learn and sensed that I did not know what was needed to fill that void in my life.

I sincerely longed to know if God really existed or not. I wanted answers, yet the people who carried Bibles under their arm intimidated me. Some seemed fanatical. I also thought they would judge me because of how I lived; so I fled from them. However, my thirst to find out who that Creator was, that others spoke about, grew. On one occasion, I dared to listen to what the Christians were saying. I was open minded and allowed them to tell me their story. What was surprising was that they did not judge me and their explanations did not sound crazy. On the contrary, their words gave me peace.

Around that time, I met a woman named Aurelia who lived in my neighborhood that I started driving to work with. She spoke to me about her personal relationship with God. Later, she invited me to go to church with her and since I had never heard of this type of relationship with God, I accepted the invitation. Of course, my son's father disagreed. He said that Aurelia did not know anything about life, despite her giving us wise counsel on how to improve our relationship both as a couple and as parents. My boyfriend did not allow anyone to tell him what to do and he completely hardened his heart to the idea of attending church. In his mind, he was doing everything correctly. His pride and blindness were so great that although his world and life were incrementally becoming more entangled and problematic, he was not able to admit his mistakes.

After the terrible accident, where he almost lost his life –when it was clear that God was giving him a second chance by leaving him alive– this would have been the time to learn and change his way of thinking and living. Many people visited him to talk about God with him, read the Bible and clarify what it entailed to establish a relationship with Him. He was never interested. On my side, the more I learned about God the more I wanted to know Him. It was a feeling of peace that kept growing in me, slowly but firmly. I would go with Ms. Aurelia to the Bible studies at every opportunity and requested God to teach me more; I wanted to be a good mother to guide my son and offer him a happy and healthy environment.

One day, while seated in church, I was overcome with feelings of emptiness and sadness. Nothing had changed in my life externally or visibly, so I asked God to fill me with His love. However, I felt unworthy; I did not feel I deserved it and did not believe He would do it. That day, the pastor made an altar call for people who wanted to establish a relationship with God. I did not think twice about coming forward, I wholeheartedly desired this. That night, after inviting Christ to take the reins of my life as Absolute Lord and Savior, something happened to me that changed me forever. For the first time, I felt clean and free. I experienced love. It was a different love that I had never experienced before. Though circumstances at home remained the same, I felt free from the weight of responsibility and guilt. I understood that what was happening was not only dependent on me. I clearly comprehended that my son's father also needed to change for our relationship to work. I felt strengthened and full of peace. As a woman and a mother, I began to see life in a new way. I became convinced that there really was another way to live. Nevertheless, contrary to what I expected the more my relationship with

God grew, the more problems I had with my son's father. Now there was another difference between us, he wanted nothing to do with church and was offended if I attended.

Now I understood that God wanted a better life for the three of us. However, since God is a gentleman, He does not force anyone to establish a relationship with Him –one that can transformation that person and make him free. I constantly prayed, asking God to guide us. With time, I realized that to continue living under the same roof with my son's father was only putting us at risk, because the war at home continued to escalate. On weekends, when I got back from church my son's father would be drunk and would act violently. I ignored him and when he saw the peacefulness with which I responded to his insults, he would get even angrier. On certain occasions he would take me by the neck and push me against the wall in an attempt to force me to answer his questions as to why I was attending church against his will. He said they would brainwash me there. He did not understand what was going on inside of me. I no longer felt alone or desperate. God was filling the deep emptiness in my being. I had found my Heavenly Father, in whom I felt unconditionally loved and protected!

I remember how disappointed I was in the men that had been a part of my life, up until that point. Since the moment I had placed my trust in my son's father, I felt as if at any moment I could experience a tragedy due to his unwise decisions and his addiction to alcohol, which only became stronger with the passing of time. I was confused; I wanted to help my son's father to abandon that lifestyle, yet at the same time I knew that my son's and my personal safety were on the line. I asked God to give me strength and direction to know what course of action was best. The day came when I could not continue living in constant uncertainty and fear. I concluded that even if I was not under the same roof I could still help my son's father, especially with my prayers. I perceived that God would be with me if I sought His guidance. Since the day I decided to speak directly with God, just as I do with my best friend, my life started changing in a very favorable way.

Though it was a difficult decision to make, I no longer felt alone. I now knew I could count on an all-loving and all-powerful God who would take me in his arms to heal every wound. I also realized that I had a lot of bitterness towards my own father for having abandoned me. I faced life with courage, yet my soul was full of questions and pain, which translated into bitterness. I couldn't understand how someone like my son's father, who had the opportunity of sharing with and watching his son grow beside him preferred to go have fun with his friends and flood his brain with alcohol; causing him to not think or feel and literally not to live, but vegetate.

I concluded that I did not have control over anyone else other than myself and that one day I would give an account of my actions. So I placed all of my questions before God and made specific decisions to move forward with my son. I focused on the new and beautiful things that God was showing me. Before having this beautiful relationship with my Heavenly Father, I had attempted to fill my internal void by going to parties. The interaction with some people was enjoyable, but we never spoke of deeper things and I would leave without answers or peace. Besides, my son's father also attended these parties where he would get drunk and fight with me. We would end up arguing with each other in front of other people who were with us. The truth is that I was tired of that atmosphere.

I have never repented of my new relationship with God, because I am conscious he is beside me all the time and that I have direct access to Him 24 hours a day, 7 days a week. My heavenly Father is not too busy and I never have to ask for appointments. I don't have to go through a secretary or bribe her to be able to speak with the King. I just have to communicate with Him who can do all things in the quietness of my soul. God is the only one that does not fail us and defends us in the situations we face. My relationship with Jesus is the best relationship I have ever experienced in life. My father Reynaldo was not with me during my childhood when I needed him most; however, God never abandoned my family or me. Looking back, I can see how He protected and helped mother pull through with so many children.

What is amazing is that God has a purpose for every person. It is not that He brings bad things into our life, the truth is that he gave everyone free will and responsibility to exercise self-determination. It is us as individuals who freely choose to damage other beings, because we ignore the good we could do and how much happiness we could derive from our healthy, positive, actions. God allows our decisions and their consequences because He gave the reins of the world to the men and women he created. You and I can make this world a horrible place or a paradise. Why do we blame Him for all our misfortune and suffering? Why don't we analyze our own decisions and those of the people around us to better understand where the blame and responsibility really lies? Besides, why don't we recognize that there is also the force of evil in the world, which is another significant element contributing to the chaos, death and destruction around us?

So, who do you we depend on for favorable changes to take place? Change begins in the mind. Do we want to continue on the path we are on or do we want to change? We can attempt it on our own; however, only to inevitably return to the habits and traditions that dominate us. It is much more productive to have a close relationship with God and ask Him to give us the desire and the power to change.

Before, I used to blame God and my father for all the tragedies that I lived. It is true that father's decisions affected us greatly; nevertheless, I also realize that I also made many mistakes and lived without including God in my plans and decisions. God is seeking us throughout our lifetime, but it is we who move farther or closer to Him. Also, I didn't listen to mother when she gave me wise advice. In spite of these decisions, as most of us tend to do, I dared to blame God for all my suffering. It was difficult to recognize that I have caused many negative consequences as a result of my erroneous decisions.

In the midst of my ignorance, something significant that God did was that He melted away the bitterness I had towards my father and I was able to forgive him. I may never know exactly what happened but now I have peace because I did all that was in my power, attempting to find him. The resentment I felt has vanished and I love him. I remember the beautiful actions he had and the time he spent with me.

No one can fully comprehend all of the situations that befall them or the reasons why God allows them to happen, yet it is evident that His care and provision miraculously supplies our needs. Also, God has opened doors and continues teaching me each day. I have felt his comfort in the midst of problems and I am astonished with his constant love. Perhaps, you are not able to perceive God in a more realistic and personal way. My intention is not to convince you to change your religion, since having an intimate relationship with God is not a matter of religion. What I would like is to motivate you to talk and communicate with Him, like we do with someone we love. We can do so with the confidence and assurance that He listens and realize that when we ask Him to intervene in our reality, He does. You can have the conviction that He is profoundly interested in the details of your life and wants the best for you.

For many years, I believed the only thing I needed to be happy was a stable family where there was no abuse, and where there was financial stability. This illusion tumbled to the floor when I learned that you need much more than this. The acceptance and peace that we all seek does not come through social and economic status. Deep, abiding peace is one of the results of the love relationship that flows from a person with their Creator. When we make peace with our Creator, many situations in our life take on new meaning.

We can discover the purpose that God has with each of us this enables us to find greater happiness because we learn what we are here on earth for. This knowledge gives us light to know how we fit in, with our talents to make this world a better place than we found it. Of the most important things I have learned is that God loves us ALL and that He is not just sitting there waiting to whack us with a whip like some people would lead us to believe. On the contrary, what He wants is for us to experience His deep love, His forgiveness and the transformation that he can bring about in each one of us. This experience has revolutionized my life as well as my family's.

Reflection

Who is God for you? Is He simply a force or energy for you? Dear reader, I invite you to connect with the greatest power in the universe: your Creator. I am not speaking about religion or rituals but of the All-powerful Spirit who created everything you see and what you can't see as well. Though He is spirit, He is real.

1. *The first step is to comprehend that God is a Spirit. You cannot see Him, just like you can't see television, radio or telephone waves; nonetheless, they are there. We need receptor antennas to receive or capture those signals. Likewise, you need to learn to use your spiritual antenna so you can connect with God. God requests that you connect using the receptor of your spirit. How? When you speak in your mind, through your thoughts, God can hear you and you can learn to use your spiritual antennas to understand Him.*

2. *Then, the next step is that you must be totally sincere and truthful. You cannot deceive or lie to God… He knows your story with absolute detail, including what remains of it until you die.*

3. Though you may not believe that God exists, that is not a problem. Your lack of faith does not threaten Him. Tell Him you want to know if He is real. Ask Him to reveal Himself to you.

4. Now, invite Jesus Christ to live in you as your Savior and Lord and thank Him for forgiving you. Give him the reins of your life from here on out. In this manner, the forgiveness he bought for you over 2,000 years ago will become real.

5. Then pick up a Bible. This book cannot be read as any other, from beginning to end. It is better to start with a portion of the Psalms, Proverbs, or one of the Gospels: Mathew, Mark, Luke, or John. Since God is the author, ask Him to help you understand His book and reveal himself to you.

6. He promises he will respond and rewards those who seek Him (Hebrews 11:6).

7. Then, seek Him in spirit and in truth in your heart and establish a new habit of speaking to the only true God daily, preferably when you are alone and without interruptions.

8. This sincerity on your behalf is what God desires. He loves you more than you can imagine and will use creative and loving ways for you to understand Him. Wait and see what will begin to happen. The closer and more constant your relationship with God is, the more your confidence will grow and the results of your connection with Him will be noticeable in your thoughts, feelings, and life.

13

TRULY, A NEW LIFE

Within my mind and heart, my wounds began to heal.

For a long time, I really did not intend to start another relationship with anyone. I was willing to wait until I found the prince of my dreams. I was no longer the naïve, adolescent ready to believe in love at first sight or raise my hopes up with illusions or fantasies based on someone who crossed my path telling me they loved me. I wanted to overcome my past and someday marry a man who sincerely loved my son and me. Nevertheless, for the time being I dedicated time dreaming about that future, but with my feet on the ground. I feared bringing a man into our lives that Milton would reject or that this new man would not love my son. I would not tolerate this, because what was most important for me was Milton's happiness. I decided that before being a woman, I was a mother first and this is how I would live. I learned this from mother.

During this time, I worked assembling automobile parts. Though the job provided for us, I did not want to remain there for a long time. My aspirations were to work in an office. This is when I met Giovanni, a quiet, peaceful young man who did not flirt with the girls or look at them suggestively. When I first spoke with him, I thought he was conceited; as if he believed he could conquer any woman he desired. He was from El Salvador, like my son's father and I imagined he had the same bad habits. How easily we judge and stereotype people, right? But really, with all that I lived through I was not ready to start another relationship. So, I ignored him. He always looked for a way to get closer to me and speak, though I remained indifferent.

Little by little, I realized I was wrong. Giovanni was a peace loving man and his friends spoke of him respectfully. He was one of the few people at the factory with some university education and he belonged to a well-known family in his country. Though his social class did not impress me, it did impress the other people that knew him.

Giovanni knew my son's father through common friends and knew something about our conflicts. Friend's tell everything and I was ashamed whenever he asked me about my life. I was surprised that he offered me his friendship and encouragement, when he saw me arriving late and depressed to work. During that time, on several occasions I asked for time off to leave and go home early because my confusion did not allow me to work in peace. I would arrive with swollen eyes from crying. I simply was not sure and did not want to make a mistake by leaving my son's father. Upon arriving at home, I would frequently speak with Milton and ask him how he felt living away from his dad. The boy would respond that although he missed his father, he was no longer afraid to come home or listen to him scream at mom. Several times he said he preferred to live away, even if in a small studio-type apartment. We did not have a spacious house any more, but we had peace and we felt secure. Milton was a mature boy and we could converse. Then, in spite of the uncertainty, our dreams kept me focused on my decision.

To avoid being depressed I needed a motivation to stop focusing or thinking about the current situation. This is why it was important to start new activities. I started going to the gym in the afternoons, after attending school where I was learning English, while my son practiced sports. Exercise helped me pull out of the depression faster. Besides, I kept attending a Christian church where I continued developing an intimate relationship with God. Here, I saw a significant change within my mind and heart. My wounds began to heal.

Little by little, we also began developing a beautiful relationship with Giovanni, who had a firm relationship with God. I began to realize we shared similar ideas in different areas. With time, we spoke about going steady. However, before accepting I proposed he meet my mother and son. This time I did not want to get emotionally involved without mother's approval. I also wanted to see how my son was going to react. At last they met and it was an enjoyable encounter. Mother had the intuition that I lacked. I remembered that because I had ignored her words and I had paid a high price for my rebellion, as did my sisters that chose not to pay attention to her.

Mother liked Giovanni right away, which was a positive sign for me. Milton's attitude towards him was also one of acceptance and inclusion, the same as mothers. I understood I had a "green light."

However, Giovanni had plans of returning to his country and I did not think it made any sense to start a relationship on those terms. Nonetheless, we continued getting to know each other and during this stage he shared a lot of time with mother and my son. We saw that the relationship worked harmoniously and while he didn't have any children of his own, he knew how to relate well with Milton. He was able to quickly win his respect and love. I observed that when he said good-bye to go home, my son did not want Giovanni to leave because he enjoyed his company so much. We all started to attend the same church. This is a very important aspect for building a home. Both sides need similar foundations; in other words, principles that are alike regarding their beliefs, goals in life and priorities. I wanted my son and I to continue growing spiritually. Thus, I needed to ensure myself that Giovanni had the same desire, independently of me; that it was important for him,not just to please or conquer me.

Yet, as in any relationship nothing is perfect. I found out that Giovanni's friends thought his mother was somewhat domineering and that she would not agree with our relationship. She had other plans for her son. Giovanni's parents lived in El Salvador and wanted him to return so he could finish his engineering degree. However, Giovanni did not want to do this and spoke to his parents about me. Surprisingly, they accepted our relationship. Months passed and we became even more in love with each other. By his side, I felt valued as well as secure and protected. I felt overwhelming peace in this relationship. I did not fear him or suffer anguish and for the first time I felt it was possible to have a healthy relationship with the opposite sex. I could even be myself without fear of rejection.

I began to lay aside other insecurities and, once again I dared to dream alongside of a man. Now my goals were bigger. Giovanni was an open-minded person and his personality generated a peaceful environment where I could grow because of the genuine love he offered me.

During the time we were getting to know each other, we shared various activities together. Our objective was to share quality time together and with my son. On occasion, the nightmares I had previously lived would come to mind and I would become afraid of being hurt once again. Several times, these feelings caused me to create barriers around my heart to the point of wanting to terminate the relationship with Giovanni. My ex-boyfriend's words regarding other men tormented me. This insecurity and fear did not allow me to accept Giovanni's serious and genuine intentions.

Whenever I felt invaded by fear I suggested we give each other time to clearly think about our goals, since I did not feel ready to move on with the relationship and needed to put distance between us. Giovanni behaved like a gentleman and supported my decision, affirming that he would never force me to do anything I did not want to do. He would respect my decision and space. This action brought me to confirm his intentions and see what was in his heart, which was completely contrary to what I had previously experienced. Finally, I concluded that I was truly learning to love Giovanni and I stopped wrestling with my doubts and absurd feelings. I buried the past and decided to walk in the present.

I constantly also struggled with cruel comments by people who judged me for having a new relationship as a separated woman. They thought I had dumped my son's father to start new adventures with other men and felt they had the right to judge my actions, while ignoring the kind of life I was leading with my ex. Frankly, I feared that Giovanni would be affected by people's comments; however, he didn't care what people said. We then decided to confront the gossip and obstacles and continue on in the relationship.

Some of my friends advised me not to take the relationship with Giovanni so seriously and so quickly. They suggested I give myself the opportunity to get to know other men and enjoy my youth to the maximum, since I had not done so previously.

I heard so many opinions that I felt confused. What helped me obtain clarity were the dreams I had. My vision was clear, I wanted to have a stable and happy home, a good father for my son, a man that was responsible and would back me up when I wanted me to improve myself intellectually. I would not have been able to attain any of this if I had relationships with people who had different goals and aspirations in life. Coming closer to God taught me that I had enormous value because I had been created in His image and I would therefore not accept any man to simply have fun with me as in times past.

After a few months, Giovanni decided to stay in the United States to continue building the relationship. We spoke of future plans together and in one year we came closer as boyfriend and girlfriend. In Giovanni's family and in the culture in which he grew –as is common in many places today– couples tend to live together under the same roof for a time to see if the relationship works out. Then, if they agree, some of them have a civil wedding. In Giovanni's family, there were few couples that had church ceremonies, so he thought it was a good idea for us to live together for awhile before getting married. On the other hand, I knew what I wanted and this was not an option for me. Having gone off to live with my son's father without the commitment of marriage, was craziness, and I was not willing to make this same mistake. I learned that without commitment and marriage vows from the beginning, a couple was basically declaring the relationship a failure before it even began. This lack of commitment makes a relationship even frailer. Giovanni did not oppose the idea of us getting married and planned to formally ask for my hand.

The day he proposed for us to marry, we could no longer imagine life without each other. Mother and Milton were extremely happy because they too believed we were made for each other. It was evident for me how mother had accepted this relationship. She could see that this man was good for me, would not mistreat me and that we could team up well together. Oh, had I listened to mother the first time how much pain I could have avoided! Although, I must admit, I would not exchange Milton for anything in this life.

We got married by the Justice of the Peace, and alongside were mother, my best friend, Giovanni's best friend and other close friends. It was an intimate ceremony. I realized I it had been worth it to take this relationship seriously and I had not made a mistake this time. I knew that Giovanni married me without worrying what people thought. He demonstrated his loyalty towards me and obedience towards God and man, by starting our union with the marriage covenant rather than simply living with me.

Knowing Giovanni has been an enormous blessing from God for my son and me. He has been a father for Milton from the beginning, loving and sincerely respecting him. Our marriage was the beginning of many goals we have achieved together. Giovanni knew the longing I had since I was a child of getting married in a church ceremony, wearing a beautiful white dress, and feeling like a princess for just one day in my life. This is why he had been saving to fulfill my wish, so that we could have that special ceremony. However, we agreed that instead we would use the funds for a down payment on a house.

Mother went to live in Ohio, where my sister, Elia, was living. She was starting to show signs of serious problems. She knew and trusted Giovanni and that my son and I were in good hands. My other five siblings were in Mexico and I had not been able to see them again. We maintained communication with them via letters and telephone. My sister Dioselina had married and had her first daughter. Mother continued to help them out financially. Dioselina was still in charge of the younger siblings showing admirable tenacity and dedication. Though our lives had slowly taken different paths, we have never lost the relationship of unity and affection we always had.

Three years after being married we had the privilege of celebrating our wedding in a church, just as I had always dreamed of. Our first son together, Dylan, had been born. He was two and Milton was already nine. The ceremony was a dream come true. My brother Gabriel walked me down the aisle and mother and Israel were present. Uncles and cousins came from Ohio. Also attending the ceremony were Giovanni's parents and family members from different parts of the country. Our Pastor and friend, Edgar Gomez, conducted the wedding which was emotional and one could perceive the prescence of a deep abiding harmony. My long, white princess style dress, adorned with small imitation diamond stones was beautiful. I also wore a crown and white veil. With all of this, my husband made me feel like that God had created me as a princess. I will never forget that magic moment. Our beautiful wedding was the fulfillment of one of the deepest longings of my life. Perhaps it is for the majority of women.

A wedding is a moment where you wear a dress that you will never wear again. It is a day in which everyone's attention is focused on the bride and a moment of personal history in which you express to all your joy for having found your Prince Charming. A wise man should realize this and enable his princess to feel valued in this regard. Love is demonstrated not just with words but with actions. This is how we celebrated, surrounded by our loved ones who shared our joy in this significant event.

Reflection

Fill yourself with courage and chose a new life. The decision is yours! The first thing you will need is to heal. For this to occur, you will need to definitely distance yourself from the people and activities that harm you and dedicate yourself to rebuilding your life. Then you will have the capacity to relive, to learn how to dream again and to seek new relationships. Discover the talents and the beauty that God has given you; develop your potential and become the marvelous person God created you to be.

1. *Open your heart! For that to happen, you need to leave your past behind, abandon bitterness, and above all, to be free you need to learn to forgive. Without forgiveness, one cannot be happy!*

2. *Make a list of all those people that have hurt you.*

3. *Ask God for forgiveness for each one of these people, whether they have hurt you or someone you love. If you decide to keep the bitterness inside, the one you are hurting the most is yourself and you may even be affecting your health. However, if you decide to forgive, you will start the healing process.*

4. *It is not a matter of "feeling" the forgiveness, but of making a decision. Those who hurt you also have serious wounds that others created in them. Though this does not justify their actions, understand that they too are broken people and do not know how to heal themselves.*

5. *Decide to give up your pain before the cross of Christ and do as He did, sincerely asking, "Father, forgive them because they don't know what they are doing" (Luke 23:34).*

6. *Do this today. Do not wait a single day longer. Now take that list where you wrote the names of each offender and after praying for each of them that God may also heal them, burn the paper.*

7. *Decide not to remember that past any more. This is one of the most liberating acts you can achieve! Experience it today.*

14

BATTLES AND ... TRIUMPHS

We are part of the problem, and also part of the solution.

Perhaps you are thinking –like I used to think– when I married Giovanni, my prince charming, that now everything in my life would be happiness and contentment. Well, that did not happen! Like many of the readers, I began a marriage after having lived a relationship of abuse that was both physical and mental and I was immersed in a mold of behaviors I didn't know how to break loose from. I did not know how to speak in a loving manner or how to live differently than I had. This led me to make many mistakes, even when Giovanni was a peace-loving and understanding person.

The truth was I didn't completely trust him. Although I loved him, I had a hidden fear of suffering, just as I did in the previous relationship. This fear did not allow me to completely surrender my love and trust to Giovanni. I had placed a barrier in my heart that did not allow me to freely express my feelings and I could not fully receive the love he offered me. The reality is that most of us enter marriage, or a romantic relationship, with our eyes closed, ignoring that we are part of the problem and also part of the solution. Each person has attitudes and behaviors that can either build up or destroy a relationship. They choose what they want to bring into the equation. In school, they don't teach us how to relate to each other or how to have differing opinions without offending, or how to reconcile with each other (among many other lessons we should have learned as children). We should have learned these behaviors at home, but they are rarely taught.

The truth is I lived with a constant distrust which manifested itself every time we had a disagreement. I was not able to cooperate with him in order to come to agreements. In spite of this, five months after we were married we planned to have our first child and I got pregnant. This pregnancy was difficult for both of us because I would often get depressed and he had never experienced so many changes all at once. Besides, this was his first child and he wasn't ready for this new phase. Who is really ready for their first child? Or even for the rest of them?

When Dylan was born, my husband's parents came from El Salvador to live with us, while Walter, my husband's brother, was already living with us. I agreed, and at the beginning everything was functioning well. Little by little, as tends to happen in most relationships, problems began to enter into the environment. Several factors occurred. It was difficult to adapt to each other's customs. Dylan, my parents-in-law's first grandson, became the center of all attention when they arrived. They became involved in all aspects of his care, because I had to return to work four weeks after he was born. My mother and father-in-law stayed home with the baby and were an enormous blessing and help to us. At the same time, we had some issues arise. My mother and father-in-law did not like that I was investing several hours after work every evening to continue my education. On the contrary, I wanted to continue in school in order to earn more money. I justified my decision on the grounds of the financial benefit for the family. In spite of this, when I decided to take classes to obtain my insurance license they backed me up, taking turns with my husband in order to care for Dylan. A few months later, they purchased their own house and went to live with my brother-in-law, Walter. When they separated from my husband, they felt as if they had lost a son and they were filled with jealousy towards me. They saw me as the guilty party, though I always treated them with affection and respect, even when I was not in agreement with some of their or decisions. It was difficult for my mother-in-law to learn to detach herself and depend less on her son, because he now had his own family. What was a blessing was that during this time my in-laws began to experience a closer relationship with God. Though it took us all some time to adapt to the changes, slowly they began to understand that they had to respect their son's life and his decisions concerning how he would raise their grandchildren and other areas of life as a couple. Finally, Giovanni placed some distance in the relationship with his parents, in a healthy and mature way. Of course, his affections did not change, but marriage implies a shift in priorities, both for husbands as well as wives. When this change does not occur, the couple's relationship suffers and can deteriorate. If couples would learn this early on in their relationship, there would be fewer problems and headaches later.

The bible is clear in its teaching that both a man and a woman must leave their mother and father's home and cleave to each other to form their new home together. From then on, they must assume their own decisions and consequences. They are no longer the responsibility of their parents. During this time, I learned many things. I realized I had to respect my husband's cultural and traditional differences and that I needed to be more willing to be an understanding woman and grow in trust towards him. To achieve this, I had to become conscious of my own flaws. In fact, one of the most difficult areas was forgiveness. The people that had harmed me had entangled me in a past that no longer existed; however, that past still affected me because I kept it alive and well, and still lived in my mind and emotions. The lack of forgiveness is like having a serpent in the house. The more it grows, the greater the risk you have of being bit with its venom.

Until I learned to forgive, I could not be free and happy in my new relationship. My husband also matured in his relationship with his parents. Though he respected and dialoged with them, he learned that as a couple, we had to resolve our own conflicts. The best of intentions to maintain a good relationship are not enough to achieve one. We had to learn to dialogue, to disagree, to find the wisest decisions for of all those involved, to receive counsel, to seek God together and to trust in each other; lessons society had never taught us. Above all, it would have been impossible to demolish the barriers that arise in a relationship without the wisdom of God. Only God in the human heart can transform selfishness and pride, which destroy unity and peace in a home, in the work place and in a community.

The key was that we were both willing to accept divine principles and allow them to lead us, instead of continuing to live in our selfish, unjust, disorganized and rebellious ways. When we realized this truth, we had come to the point of a separation. We felt angry, tired and frustrated with each other. We had beautiful children whom we deeply loved, a stable family, economic stability and health. However, it seemed as if what we had attained together was not enough. We really did not feel happy. Something was missing in our relationship. The more the emotional distance grew between us, the more we sought a logical, human solution, without it actually leading us to anything sustainable. It was at this point we started to seek God's guidance more. Having lived the previous experience with my first son's father, I couldn't understand how now that alcohol and other vices were not present it was still not possible to find emotional stability between us.

We began to learn that both of us were culpable. The simple fact was that we were imperfect beings. Having cultural and educational differences, being raised with different methods and the fact that he was a man and I was a woman were main causes for discord. All of this resulted in different ways of perceiving and understanding the world. I wanted to continue my education and obtain my title, even though it involved spending time outside of the home and was an impediment to spending more quality time with both my husband and my children. Household chores also accumulated and even though I tried to balance these, it was not enough for us to reach an agreement. At the end of each day, Giovanni would voice his frustrations over my absence or a lack of attention to him and the children.

From my logic, I thought he should be happy because I had the desire to make something of myself. With better educational training, I could obtain a better job position and earn greater income for the entire family. I did not realize that all of this would be at a great cost. The so called "better quality of life" was driving me to being careless with what I loved most: my husband and children. In a way, focusing so much on my goals was a selfish attitude, because I was placing an unjust burden on Giovanni, whom I expected to back me up in everything. This does not mean that my desire to improve myself was wrong. What I needed was to measure the cost in time, money, effort and external support that we needed. I did not realize that by focusing primarily on the material aspect, I was making the same mistake that my parents had made.

The most important thing was understanding both sides, coming to an agreement, defining how we could support each other and what was needed to balance the sacrifice that this objective required. Giovanni got tired of trying to persuade and show me that I was out of focus. He opted to keep his opinions to himself regarding my attitudes and behaviors. In other words, to a great degree he became silent. He simply did what he could to help me around the house and preferred to do the tasks to avoid discussions. What this generated was a time bomb that kept accumulating more and more pressure each day. We felt that our home was coming to an end and this was when I accepted that I was wrong in many regards. The truth was that I was the main cause of our problems now. My husband had given up and concluded that it was not worth it to continue fighting for a home where his wife was more interested in her education than in her own family.

I also realized that I was not an expressive wife, which made Giovanni feel like I really didn't love him. Though I did love him, I did not show him my sentiments for fear of him taking advantage of me and making me suffer. This situation eventually led to a communication breakdown, where we reduced dialogue to monosyllables. After that shake up, I learned to place God first. Then I continued understanding how to value and love myself, but in a balanced way, without believing me to be more or less than other people. My priorities became my husband first, followed by my children and extended family. My next priority was work, then responsibilities at church, followed by commitments in the community and finally, everything else. This order for relationships, established by God, who created the human race and knows how it functions best, eliminates internal conflicts, because we clarify our loyalties.

With that confrontation and realization that I was once again on the verge of losing my home, I purposed to change my priorities, realizing that all we had accumulated materially was not important. Then, what I wanted most was to recuperate the time I had lost with my family. I wanted to restore our relationship; even though I thought it was too late. However, I didn't give up. Instead I took responsibility for my actions and made the changes that showed my husband I truly loved him and was committed to our children and family.

Giovanni was also willing to do his part to overcome the problem. Together, with God's help and our church leaders, we were able to restore the trust and communication that a home requires. When the storm was over and we felt the relationship was improving, Giovanni had a serious motorcycle accident. This tragedy unified and showed us how fragile life is and how it can fade in seconds. We realized it was not worth it to live in a state of contention with those you love most. I now had the strength to leave my fears and resentment behind me. That incident made me value the life I shared with my husband and children and I did not want to continue making the same mistakes from the past.

From that point on, we entered into a higher level of maturity in our relationship where we supported one another so that each of us could fulfill their goals as individuals and as a team, without envy or competition. It is very clear when God says that the "two" become "one single flesh." We realized that everything we attained was ultimately for the well-being of our family nucleus.

Giovanni also learned to dedicate his life to pleasing God first, and then to dedicate himself to his family, which enables us to have a mutually satisfying relationship between us. Organizing his life with God first and not as culture propels us to, with a self-centered emphasis, helped us find balance in all the other areas. It does not mean we became perfect, and while we still make mistakes, we now resolve them in a wiser, more prudent manner, taking into consideration each other's feelings, experiences and knowledge. Above all, we learned to seek God's wisdom and guidance which are found in the principles of His Word, the Bible.

The learning continues every day. Now we know that when we reach agreements it produces stability and our children experience peace. Though our parents and siblings are very important to us, we understand that when a person chooses to marry, the immediate family, husband or wife and children, become the first priority after God. Then comes the extended family. This order is important to ensure that we assign the proper priority to everyone in our lives.

A couple's relationship is fragile and receives attacks from every angle. Evil forces desire to destroy the sacred bond between husband and wife which God established because it is the most potent way to destroy individuals, children, families and entire societies. What's more, these wicked spiritual forces also seek to destroy homes because healthy marriage represents the type of unity God desires between a man and a woman. In this bond of marriage, forgiveness, respect, cooperation and loyalty is the best environment for a person to develop. For this reason, it is necessary to battle using prayer, as we apply biblical principles for the family to triumph.

Love is like a flower that must be cared for daily. If you water it lovingly, it will bloom and not dry up. However, this implies we l-e-a-r-n to love, more and more with the unconditional love that God loves us. We will not love perfectly, but we can learn to love less selfishly. This demands a decision on our behalf to totally surrender, without expecting the other half to do anything to deserve it. It means to accept and love a person as they are. This is a behavior that we learn, yet the vast majority of people only know how to love when it offers them an advantage, or personal gain, or when they want something in exchange. However, we were not called to be other people's judges, but to stretch out our hand to help each other change any destructive attitude and behavior. If we seek to know God better and walk with other people who are also committed to Him, we can enjoy a deep abiding peace and live the reward of the beautiful union that marriage can be. Three people make up the marriage of those who love God. In the equation is each member of a couple, plus the Holy Spirit. When we invite Him to be the main partner of this union and we are willing for Him to work in each one of us, the marriage can function quite well.

Through this book, I have wanted to share my personal experiences and encourage you not to quit. Dear reader, dare once again to dream and enjoy life. Learn to respond, not ignoring your mistakes or denying them; not reacting out of anger but facing them and working to change behaviors you exhibit that are not constructive for you or for those around you.

First, recognize that if you are facing difficulties and even tragedies in your life, the majority of these are consequences of the decisions you, your parents, or those who raised you have made. You should not blame your Creator; He made us all free. God's will is not for us to suffer. On the contrary, He wants to guide us so we may develop a character that nurtures and blesses others. He has thoughts of peace and well-being for you, but you need to take steps to come closer to Him.

I am grateful for the many opportunities that God has granted me. Although my son Milton has spent the majority of his life away from his biological father, he has never lacked love. When we separated, my son's father continued living in the same city. A few years later, he sold the house we had purchased and went to live in California with his family. He never remarried or had any other children. He visits Milton and we communicate regarding important decisions about our son. I also have a beautiful relationship with his sisters and mother, whom I deeply appreciate. They love my son and care for him. Though I would love to affirm that my son's father is free from the vice of alcohol, this is not so. He continues to live with the same problem. Every time Milton finds out his father has had a new difficulty, he asks me to pray for him so that God will work in his life. I am happy they have a good relationship and that the wounds of the past have healed.

My son can also count on his adoptive father that admires, loves and respects him. Giovanni has been exceptional with him. Our children Dylan and Kayler are also growing up surrounded by our love, care, example and dedication. I know now we are better prepared to teach our children. We know that to honor and love God is the most important element in establishing family relations. Each day, we ask for understanding to educate and guide our children on paths of righteousness and respect. Besides, we are motivating them to study beyond high school until they finish their university training, since this is one of the values in our home. As a couple, we continue learning to care for and cultivate our marriage so that it will flourish in every stage.

When facing conflicts, one has three options: to learn from them and decide to change favorably, to close yourself up and continue blindly in the same direction, or becoming worse. This is called, not being teachable, or falling into defeat! Fools do that, those who believe they know it all and whose pride does not allow them to question themselves. I invite you to become wise and to seek God daily. He has answers you can't even imagine, if you will simply make the time to speak with Him. When we have learned from a conflict, we can make decisions that produce positive consequences, that are fair, that edify and produce joy in us, as well as in those around us.

... AND TRIUMPHS

If you say you believe, but do not act upon what you believe then it is simply an improbable illusion, not real and active faith. After our reconciliation, Giovanni continued working at the factory where we met and I continued learning how to operate computers during my free time, with the dream that one day I would be able to work in an office. With Lupita, another woman with similar ideals as me, we would spend hours planning our future. We appreciated our current job but wanted to continue improving ourselves. She spoke English very well and taught me quite a lot. She was not envious and shared her knowledge so that I could also reach my goal. Several fellow workers, who were full of jealousy and bitterness and desired to see us fail, overheard our plans and scoffed at us. Their insinuations did not bother us because we were clear on what we wanted.

In the factory, my bosses saw the interest I had in learning and several times, they took me into the office to file documents. But as is common in every place, the envious are not absent from the scene and several co-workers opposed this action. They requested that they too, be taken to work at the office. They raised such a controversy that our supervisors decided not to take anyone. I was able to experience the jealousy, competition and envy among those of our own Hispanic community. Sadly, instead of helping and supporting each other, and contributing to the growth and development of other Latin-Americans in this country, many people prefer to pull others down to advance themselves. They ignore that all of those who want to, can improve themselves in different fields and with varying degrees of knowledge. There is room for all! It is not like this among other cultures that demonstrate more unity and support so that each member can get ahead.

Before marrying Giovanni, the factory terminated my contract. However, instead of feeling anguish I was happy with the news, thinking it would be a good opportunity to find my desired job. With persistance, I finally I got my High School diploma. Now I had both a temporary work permit as well as my Social Security card. These were important achievements in order to obtain an office job. I was clear on the fact that I had come to this country with the purpose of helping my siblings, but along the way I learned new things that could help me fulfill my other goals. The truth is that I miss my brothers and sisters and the warmth and culture of my people; nonetheless, this country has offered me many opportunities that I value and has helped me grow; nonetheless, I have not forgotten my roots.

Within a short time, God opened the doors for me to become a cashier in a bank despite my having no experience. I was hired only because I spoke English and Spanish. It was evident that the time spent preparing myself had not been in vain. Initially, when I heard about this position I was discouraged because I lacked experience; however, Giovanni encouraged me to go to the interview. Five other people were also present. I felt happy and thought this job was for me, yet I was surprised when they chose me. The managers that chose me affirmed that I seemed positive and kind. I know it was God's favor that placed the attitude they were looking for in me. There were other girls, perhaps better trained than I, but either they lacked God's favor, or it wasn't His plan for them.

I am aware that training is very important and so I had acquired computer knowledge, which was a prerequisite for the job. Although I knew both languages, I had never worked at a bank. I did what was in my power to do and from then on, I saw God working in what I could not do, giving me grace and favor with the interviewers.

In 2001, I began working for an insurance agency. They hired me to make calls to Spanish speaking people offering free life, auto and home insurance estimates. They gave me a thick yellow page book and instructed me as to how I was to make the calls to people with Spanish surnames in alphabetical order. To achieve this, I sat at the back part of the office in a cubicle for three hours, four days a week and carried out this marketing function.

A few months later, the Hispanic clients were noticeably growing. Therefore, my bosses increased my work hours and my responsibilities. The truth be told, I enjoyed the work and took every opportunity to learn as much as I could about processing contracts. I also interpreted for Hispanic clients during their appointments.

Although it was not an easy decision, because I liked my job at the bank, I eventually decided to take the position at the insurance company because I realized it could mean a better future, greater challenges and the possibility of greater growth. I felt I was learning English faster because I was practicing it daily. In addition, I had attained my dream of working in an office and had left the factory environment.

After almost a year, the insurance company offered me a full-time job increasing my salary, thus compensating what I was earning at my second job at the bank. I accepted the proposal and left my cashier's job to focus exclusively on the insurance company. Day by day, my knowledge increased regarding the different insurance processes. I learned how to process contracts, payment transactions, make adjustments, and even how to market the business.

Two years later, the owner offered me the opportunity of obtaining my State Insurance license, which would allow me to become an Insurance Agent. Thus, I would be trained and authorized by the state to process new contracts on my own. I made the effort and studied hard and with the owner and manager's help I obtained the license I had longed for. It took me seven attempts to pass the P&C test, and five to pass the L & H test, but I persisted until I obtained my goal. Right away, they opened up a new branch in another city where they sent me to manage and develop the clientele in that region. They also sent another bilingual employee to occupy the position of Consumer Services, while I processed new contracts. This is how my experience as manager of an insurance agency began.

Several times, when the owners changed locations or opened a new agency, they would send me to establish it. Once it was established and had grown, they would assign me a new project. Nine years went by in which I enjoyed every challenge within that industry and I continued learning and feeling more sure of what I was doing.

Dave, the owner, Rhonda, the manager, and I, came to feel great mutual appreciation for each other. Though they did not speak Spanish, they supported me in learning English and they taught me everything relevant to the insurance business. I never felt discriminated against for not speaking their language perfectly. On the contrary, they encouraged me to continue learning and they made me feel privileged because I could speak two languages.

On occasions, I could see the opposite attitude with some clients that would call and get upset when they heard my accent. They did not want a person with a foreign accent to service their policies. Perhaps they believed that because I didn't speak English well, my brain also had an accent and I did not understand my job well. People confuse one thing with another and they discriminate rapidly. Initially, I felt sad and frustrated, but Dave and Rhonda defended me and in spite of what people said, they continued delegating work to me and encouraged me to continue learning. They affirmed that the ones who were wrong were the other people who were myopic and closed minded and who judged without knowing a person's capabilities. To this day, I hold a deep gratitude toward them for what I learned and for the beautiful attitude they always demonstrated towards me.

This opportunity in the insurance company was a wonderful occasion and blessing that I received and enjoyed. I learned how to better relate to others, to know people from different countries, cultures, traditions and characteristics. In spite of all the positive elements, something started to change in my way of thinking. I felt as if there were no more challenges to conquer and my daily tasks became a routine. My salary was not the problem, I earned an acceptable wage; however, I wanted something more. I sought a greater challenge, a new vision in which I could apply my creativity and all that I had learned.

Then, I contemplated the possibility of opening a new business in another field. Perhaps it would be in sales, yet I had not defined the type of industry

I was interested in. Various people suggested business opportunities that seemed interesting. I even tried out some businesses that, although they were interesting were not what I really wanted. I also attained my license as a Real Estate Agent, after taking the State test also five times; however, I did not practice the profession.

Because I already knew the insurance industry, I thought I should start my own business; nonetheless, I hesitated for several months. I wondered if this was really what I should do or if it was better to apply the knowledge I had acquired in another business.

I began to pray to God asking for His direction, but I was confused and all the ideas I heard seemed good. Suddenly, conflicting situations started to occur in the agency I was managing. The market started to change and created restrictions in my service to the community I had been working with for years. Simultaneously, the owner called me to a meeting and gave me the opportunity of choosing whether to discontinue working with the market I served –because the rules had changed and it was no longer acceptable for the companies we represented– or they would impose restrictions in the system to process only a percentage of the contracts. This modification reduced our new clients at least by 50%.

When considering these changes, I was not concerned about a possible salary reduction as I had generated business relationships with an ample number of clients which, if I maintained, produced significant income. What bothered me the most was feeling as if my hands were tied when I had no authority to defend what I believed was just. I did not want to break the rules, but rather to implement my ideas that could help the company continue serving a needy community. I felt that due to a lack of managers and companies who provided information based on these services, they preferred to ignore those needs and evade them, instead of designing adequate ways to service this community.

It was obvious that the panic and possibility of losing it all could blind well-intentioned hearts. I feel this is what happened to the owners of the firm. One day, as I was driving to an appointment many ideas began to rush to my head. At first, they seemed to be vain and blurry ideas. I thought it was due to all that was happening, but as the days went by they became clearer. Then I asked myself, is this the opportunity that Giovanni and I have been praying for? If it were God's will, was I really prepared to assume it? Would

I know where to start?　Who could I ask to help me, give me ideas and encouragement? I had no answers to these questions. The only thing I could think with clarity was that I should move ahead to make contacts. If God was backing me up, He would open the doors.

Fear of the unknown was strong, yet I perceived God's favor. I saw that my dreams were firm and the emotion of a new challenge was stronger than the actual fear I had. As a matter of fact, I could employ the experience I had, combined with new ideas, in addition to reserved energy that was ready to explode within.

I had heard the phrase many times that when the student is ready, the teacher shows up. So I resigned and shared with my bosses the plan I had. They agreed, since they preferred to avoid conflicts with the companies that did not want to work with the market I served. They thanked me for my honesty and time I had invested developing their company.

This was a new chapter in my life. I knew it would not be easy, yet it was what I wanted to do. I started my own insurance company with the assurance I would not turn back. I burned all the bridges behind me because turning back regarding business, was not in my agenda. Now it was all or nothing. With only the experience of selling insurance policies, receiving payments and processing changes, I started to form a team of consultants in diverse areas. My husband supported me in these decisions, though not as a consultant.

I sought to surround myself with experienced people, among them were an attorney, an accountant and mentors to develop the business. I established the business name and took all the necessary steps required by the city and government to obtain legal recognition; I even wrote the business plan. Little by little, my vision took on form.

At the beginning, there were days I doubted if my plan would work. The companies I called were either not accepting new clients or required a greater number of clients than I had. Others just didn't feel I had the necessary experience to work with them.

I heard all manner of rejections, though I also won some contracts with companies that continued to push my idea forward. During this time, I received emails and calls from the previous company I had worked for asking me if I wanted to continue with my plan or if I had changed my mind and wanted to return to work with them. On certain days, that idea didn't sound bad at all, because I was under a lot of stress. However, I decided not to give up.

I kept my eyes on the dream, on what I wanted to achieve and in what my heart longed for. I had faith that it would all work out well, though I was unsure of how exactly I would do it. One day, I expressed my fears to an employee, that upon termination of the existing contracts and not having new companies to transfer clients to, we would have to close.

She suggested I call a company where her friend had worked; it that was a large and well-known company. Perhaps they were recruiting new agents. She found out the agent's number –who was the district manager– and I hesitated to call because I figured if small companies had rejected me, a larger company would have even more reason to reject me. In spite of this, I encouraged myself, called them and was immediately granted an interview. The recruiter was surprised with the business plan and vision I had. He immediately coordinated another meeting with Tom Gregwer, the district manager, who saw us a week later. By the end of that meeting, Tom was convinced that our agency was what his company was looking for.

With no further delay, they began their investigation and I and my company were accepted by Farmers Insurance. The opportunity was greater than I had realized. I would have access to all types of contracts and they worked with the market that we wanted to help. I was placed as a reserve agent and one month later, my team and I had attained the required level. I was recognized as a professional career agent, which meant I not only would receive bonuses and growth promotions, but would also participate receiving support to finance fixed as well as employee expenses.

In conclusion, on January 2011 I opened my own insurance agency with Farmers along with 2 full-time staff members. Because of the excellent relationships, and recognition I had in the community as an insurance agent, people started approaching our company for their insurance needs from day one. We continued surpassing previous growth levels and as a result, Farmer's has compensated us with favorable bonuses. We won competitions in less than half the time of other agencies and we have received trophies for our achievements in educational campaigns and for providing adequate protection to our clients. I have the joy of sharing that three months after I joined Farmers I obtained first place in the growth of new sales in a contest where more than 15,000 agents participated from all over the country. We had the opportunity of attending a recognition ceremony for our achievement in California along with one of my workers and friend, Blanca Delgado. The top 26 agents with the greatest growth in the country attended and one of them won a classical vehicle.

Tom Gregwer and the District office supported my staff and I from the begining. I have received their continued and ongoing support not just as an agent but as my business consultants. We have truly built a wonderful partnership and have helped create jobs. Because of this phenomenal relationship, our Insurance Agency has been the recipient of paid trips and various awards given by The Farmers and its group of companies in recognition of our sales efforts, growth and market expansion.

This is only the beginning. With every step we take and every achievement we reap in this area and others, my vision expands as the days go by. With God's grace and protection I will continue to enjoy every challenge that comes our way, believing I don't have failures, but challenges which help me grow and reach other levels.

What lies ahead is not easier, but greater and more exciting than what has thus occurred. Only God knows what he has prepared for me and I chose to believe Him each day and act based on that belief. If you say you believe, but don't act on that belief, then it is just an illusion and not real faith.

I have narrated what happened so that it may serve as inspiration for all of those who have a dream. Your dream may be to study, start your own business, get married, travel, become a doctor or bring a new idea to the market. The possibilities are endless. I want to especially motivate women, to not allow anything to intimidate or stop you. Fix your eyes on the goal and do not stop until you achieve it. If God gives you a dream, He will also give you the tools, people, knowledge, money, time and strength to achieve it! However, you need to take the steps to recognize Him in all of your plans, because it is God who grants lasting success and happiness!

The image we have given, in general, of our Hispanic culture in the United States is one of hard working people, who are honest overall. More than titles and positions, what is most important is that we can leave footprints wherever we go that may also inspire others not just towards personal good and family well-being, but also toward achieving collective well-being.

Today, I continue reading and preparing myself to fulfill whatever purpose God has for me in the future, so that when a door opens up I can be ready to take on new challenges and responsibilities. What I most enjoy, besides singing and reading is motivating people to develop their talents. I am passionate about seeing others achieve their dreams, just like I am doing. I want them to see that it is possible. Every opportunity that comes your way implies struggles, challenges, difficulties and also joys.

Likewise, these experiences strengthen you. The Bible says that whoever is faithful in small things will be given greater responsibilities. Learn to do well what you have now and train yourself in what you like, to assume the future with passion. It is never too late to start our dreams, we are never too old to fly and go beyond the clouds. If we discover what God has put within us and are willing to make the effort to achieve them, the experiences that await us will be greater than the current ones. Are you ready to take on these challenges?

After all the confusion, trip ups, voids and pains through which I have gone, I would have never imagined my life almost two decades later. Where would this farm girl be and with whom? What would she be doing? The opportunities that the Lord has given me are many and for these I am most grateful. Who would have imagined how happy I would be today and the internal peace that I have?

Though I could not find my earthly father, my search enabled me to find my Heavenly Father, the beginning and end of all things created, who fulfills me like no human being. My personal relationship with Him is the source of inspiration for all that I do. His light guides and teaches me wisdom to walk in this world. Knowing Him has allowed me to accept the love of a Father and I have found tranquility in my spirit.

I am also committed with a community of faith and they are committed with me. Here I give and receive support and strength from many people. We offer each other love and practical help when needed. In this community we learn to live less egotistically, closer to God's plans for humanity and to live in harmony.

Because of this intimate relationship with God, each one of the members of my family, mother, siblings, nieces and nephews, husband and children now live quite a different life. We have understood that we don't have to destroy ourselves, or live in a state of permanent war with each other. When we allow Jesus to reign in our lives a miracle truly occurs. Today we celebrate a great victory, thanks to the transformational work that Christ has achieved in each of us. However, during the learning phase, which certainly never ends, I have often asked myself, why is it that most of my sisters and I have been victims of psychological and physical abuse? Now, I understand that since we were girls we lived this same pattern in our home and subconsciously we thought that this was normal. In addition, we made decisions that were not wise or beneficial for us. Therefore, we suffered the consequences of our own actions.

Every decision has consequences, be they positive or negative. This is why it is important not to react crazily, basing our decisions on the emotions of a moment. Every action and decision would turn out better if we made it a habit to first consult our Heavenly Father, who knows all things before they occur. It is not a matter of consulting a warlock to look into his crystal ball and deceive people into believing they know the future. We would do much better if we learned to take into consideration the One who knows the past, present and future. He can truly teach us to navigate every situation that comes our way. Learn that you can avoid terrible consequences and mistakes by consulting God before acting!

Today, I comprehend that nothing is perfect in life, yet one can enjoy it much more if we accept our flaws and adopt an open attitude when we are faced with criticism; and if we decide to change behaviors that may be impossible for us to change, but not for God. We can learn to forgive those who hurt us and to develop the capacity to motivate the people with whom we live with our words and example. Our micro world –that of the people in circles closest to us– would be so much different if we lived this way.

Reflection

Dear reader, I invite you to align your thoughts with God's: believe Him, follow Him and obey Him. I do not promise you the absence of pain; however, I do promise you an adventure in self-discovery and unparalleled growth in all dimensions or life where you allow His touch and unconditional love. Ultimately, proximity to Him will lead you to profound peace, security and hope. Do you accept this invitation?

One of the most significant achievements my family has made is that we will make a difference in our children's future generations. We have broken the chains of abuse, ill treatment, chauvinism, alcoholism, adultery... and we have prayed for God to bless our future generations. Remember that when a person has a truly committed relationship with God, they live in a way that is noticeably different. Not that they are perfect, but their life reflects values that promote the positive, kind, sincere, love that is not fake and manifests enduring peace, solidarity, mutual support and generosity. The lives of our children are now marked by a different pattern of coexistence and we will leave them a greater legacy than any material thing.

This is not free; there is a cost. The price that is required is learning and applying the healthy standards of the Kingdom of Light and renouncing the kingdom of darkness and evil that harms other people and us. The patterns of life that we see many people living bring pain and destruction. To seek a life like Jesus taught requires courage, decision, willingness and commitment, which you can develop, if you want to! You start by wanting to do so and making a personal decision to be different. This decision, motivated by your free will, creates an internal environment which will desire to open up and connect with the source that can achieve a transformation in you. A healthy mind and emotions that develop with time produces changes in our home and no doubt also in the community and society where we live. In this manner, we will have changed our environment, and at least our microcosm. Are you ready to begin a sustainable change? What is hindering you from doing so?

15

KEY LESSONS

At some point your life will be like an open book, composed of chapters with your daily experiences, circumstances, challenges and how you responded during these times. All people have faced suffering and conflict, as well as joys and opportunities during different stages of their lives. However, in the midst of these events, we can choose to either develop our capabilities or sink in a sea of negativism, fear and depression. Life is like a series of exams. Are you passing these with good grades? Are you learning the lessons that life is teaching you?

We begin our story with the family into which we are born, under the varying socioeconomic, cultural, religious, technological and political factors that mark us. Immersed in that specific context, we are the result of countless decisions– those we have made and also incalculable numbers of decisions that our ancestors have made before us. No doubt, our ancestors have defined a portion of our destiny. When we were young, our personal perception depended on others and how they viewed us. Yet we mature to the stage where we attaineded consciousness of how we behave as individuals. From there on, every decision we make builds up or tears down our own future and the future of the children we may have. The sum of all these decisions –others as well as our own– make up what we are today. Likewise, the sum of our decisions today is what we are becoming and what we decide tomorrow will be what we will develop into in the future. It is that simple.

Therefore, do not take lightly your activities, pastimes, the disciplines you acquire (whether sports, musical or artistic). Pay attention to the environments you frequently visit, what you see and listen to and whom you decide to connect with –intellectually, physically and occupationally. ALL of these contribute to the building blocks that assemble your character and values. Inevitably, from this circle of influences, you derive your heroes and idols; the people who we tend to imitate. Subsequently, depending on who our idols are, they will influence what we write in the book of our life whether positive or negative. Therefore, watch with whom you associate since these influences

–people, movies, music, websites…– will to a great degree, define the goals you set for yourself and even your achievements.

Here are some keys that may help you continue your journey or help pull you out of stagnation mode.

Key #1. Get close to (listen to, observe, imitate) the people whom you want to be like.

A particular characteristic of the book of our life is that at the end, unlike what an author is able to do with a piece of paper, our experiences are not erasable. A paper book, before it is sent out for printing undergoes a process of multiple revisions and changes; one can delete and add paragraphs… not so in the book of our life. Perhaps the current version of your book brings tears to your eyes and at other times laughter. The truth is that neither tears or strong reproaches can change what has already happened. What we've done, in other words the past, is irrevocably engraved. Nevertheless, be encouraged!

Key #2. As long as your heart is beating, the present and the future have yet to be written. Focus on the present and make an effort to find all that you were created to be!

Though many aspects were predetermined before our birth, not all of them were. We were created with a free will, with the capacity to freely choose our preferences. In contrast with animals that function basically by instinct, humans have the use of reason and a tremendous capacity to deliberately alter their circumstances. Therefore, you can change and become responsible for your current situation, without blaming others.

Key #3. Decide to change what you don't like about yourself by taking different actions than you have in the past, so that your results can be different.

Among the most important actions we can take is to learn from each situation in our life as well as from other people's lives. Maintain an apprentice attitude, in order to make better decisions and eliminate the same mistakes that have harmed yourself and others. I once heard a phrase that helped me deal with adverse circumstances in a proactive manner. The saying affirms that when we trip over a problem, we could have encountered a treasure because if we learn from it, it will help us rise to a higher level of understanding. This requires an open attitude, one willing and desirous to learn in order to triumph. The person that does not learn from their mistakes does not generate changes and therefore lives deceiving themself.

Key #4. Make it your purpose to discover more of the abilities and skills that God gave you. Then ask yourself, am I using them to be a blessing to those around me? What is hindering me?

Everyday is another opportunity to add a new and beautiful page to the book of your life that can be full of achievements, satisfactions and experiences that will make you and others happy. You can especially make a contribution to the many people that need your knowledge, encouragement, support, contacts, ideas and experience. Thousands of people have experienced a deep and unequaled sensation of happiness when they serve others who have fewer opportunities than they do. To live your life to the fullest potential, use your talents in every opportunity. Ultimately this can be defined as loving others.Serving others will enable you to grow at the spiritual, intellectual, physical, and social levels. When we share our talents, we realize they are a gift from heaven.

Key #5. Ask God to teach you to forgive so you will truly be free.

Everyone that leaves negative imprints in our heart could make us prisoners of pain in our own mind and feelings. If your mind is full of resentment and a lack of forgiveness, you will not be able to be happy, because you are emotionally chained down. That lack of forgiveness, be it toward oneself, God, other people or circumstances, diminishes the necessary energy to reconstruct and enjoy the present. In addition, what binds a person to another, besides their physical presence, is the control that the other person may exert over one's emotions and thoughts! Some people continue allowing this soul tie, even after the other person has left or died! Forgiveness is a decision, not a feeling. Therefore, when we choose to forgive we liberate ourselves of the chains that oppress us.

Key #6.

Learn to live conscious of every decision you make and the impact it can have tomorrow on yourself and others.

Every circumstance that comes our way has a purpose and a reason for occurring. God desires to reveal His love, kindness, mercy, and beauty to us. We need not feel anguish. Instead, we can redirect our attention and entrust every situation in the hands of our Heavenly Father. We will enjoy peace when we understand that we only need to do our part the best we can and He will take care of the rest. Although it may not seem like it at times, God is on His throne. He will govern the universe forever, as well as the destiny of nations, people and nature. God does not force anyone to action yet he knows what people will do before they do it. We can dream, ask for His wisdom and guidance, and then rebuild and sow but with His strength.

Key #7. Remember it does not depend on you to win the game, just to play it as best you can with what you have. Then leave ALL of the consequences in God's hands, because the game is not over yet.

Another valuable element is to constantly reformulate our goals so we will not stagnate. Our goals are like a lake that needs fresh water to keep from drying out or getting contaminated. Every day, the lake consumes a certain amount of water and requires cleaning from the bacteria that enter it. If we don't do this, toxins that kill living beings will accumulate. Water is like the knowledge we must add on a daily basis: knowledge of God, of people, and of the world. The bacteria or trash, are are like the bad experiences and negative relationships we have, along with the mistakes and harmful reactions we generate. Before finalizing each day, take some time in God's presence to empty the trash from your lake by analyzing your thoughts, feelings and actions. Then define new goals for the next day. Fill your lake with pure water by aligning yourself with the most potent source of the universe: your Creator. He can achieve in and through you a beautiful future.

Key #8. Next, clarify what success means for you. To define our concept of success is valuable because if we feel successful, we feel happier.

Surely, to be successful is not to vegetate or merely exist without purpose, day after day. However, the answer to this question varies depending on the stage each person is in and what they are seeking in life. There are principles that determine a greater quality of life. You can start by answering the question, what do you want from life? Your own well-being? The well-being of others? Both? Let's talk first about short term success. For me, a successful day is...

> ...to have taken advantage of that day, giving the best of myself to others

... to play and enjoy time with those I love

... to feel healthy, in other words to have taken care of my body with adequate and sufficient nourishment, rest and exercise

... to learn new things

... to challenge myself and advance towards my goals, studies and work...

... to feel I have internal harmony and am in permanent dialogue with my Creator

... to have peace with those around me (family, neighbors, friends... co-workers)

... to create something enjoyable to see and hear, (a new dish, song, poem, drawing...)

... to have not hurt or negatively affected others

... to destroy attitudes such as pride, resentment, envy, coveteness and hate... which can lead to erroneous actions

... to contribute to the community and country where I live through my work, service and other forms of giving

... to make the lives of those I appreciate or don't even know, pleasant and joyful

I could go on. This is only an example, with no order or priority. Then if we live the majority of our days coming closer to the fulfillment of our concept of success, achieving goals that build up and make others and myself joyful, we will have written a successful book of our life that day. So define what happiness and success mean to you.

Key #9. Stop hiding behind excuses. Perhaps you think you are not living the life you desire because you have not had the education or opportunities you wanted.

Allow me to say that this is NOT a reason for you to give up. It is time to search and keep searching. Perhaps you need to redefine yourself until you find your purpose, your talents and that which produces deep satisfaction for you! Most people who do not reach their dreams hide behind excuses. They allow disappointment, the lack of discipline, tiredness or the lack of motivation on behalf of others… to defeat them and they stop searching for their dreams in more adequate places. Surely, one of the most paralyzing elements is to just stand there looking and complaining because of all you lack! This attitude immobilizes us on the road to reaching our goals. We have so much to learn, especially from people who have incredible stories of how they have overcome. We can learn only when we stop focusing on ourselves. There are people who were born with physical handicaps, like my aunt Lico, people with serious health obstacles and others that have had to live in situations of war, hunger or rejection… Nevertheless, many of them have attained greater achievements than people who are healthy and have more opportunities. When we are born with good health and overflowing options, we frequently do not value them the same way as people who do not have them. Don't complain or conform to your current situation.

Key #10. Necessity itself can propel you to develop precisely what you need to succeed. A deep want or problem can frequently lead us to a great opportunity! Therefore, do not fear. Take on whatever it is, but do it with the help of heaven!

May your book not be a cheap copy of another, or one that will make the reader constantly cry. For those who take the time to read it, may your book be original and contribute vision and critical elements that will help balance other's perspectives and may it leave a song of joy in one's heart.

My prayer for you, who are holding this book in your hands, is for you to be full of the knowledge of these spiritual truths. For the person who is listening, these truth are written in nature, in a splendorous sunset, in the musical notes of a concert that makes the heart vibrate, in the miracle of a new born baby… and also in the Bible. Besides the wonder of creation, God has ingeniously preserved through the Bible a particular message for humanity, so there need not be any confusion in the seeker.

I wish for you to open your eyes to the eternal, to the peace, love, forgiveness and holistic healing for every area of your life. Above all, I pray you will discover how exquisitely good, wise and powerful God is. Trust Him with all your heart, and do not lean on your intelligence. At the end of our earthly existence, the beginning of our story on this earth will not be as important as the journey we have taken. In other words, what we did with all we received: our abilities, talents and opportunities.

The key is how we develop and what we give in exchange. In your celestial bank account what matters will not be the material things; it will be what has eternal weight. There we make deposits using a different currency, when we do things wholeheartedly for others; not for our own benefit, not to be seen, not for the compensation we could receive but simply because it was the just, right, compassionate and loving thing to do! Acquire this type of currency and make frequent deposits and you will lack nothing.

When we feed the hungry, and give water to the thirsty, when we visit the sick or those secluded in a penitentiary, when we have compassion and support those who had no other options... These actions have weight before the Maximum throne of Power. Yet let us not stop there. The greatest weight is in our own proximity and knowledge of what pleases God. Everything else will remain on this earth... Our spirit will take nothing, not one thing to that new dimension of life after death.

The most we can aspire to is that at the end of each day we can know that God smiles on us for what we have done and that we have achieved the applause of heaven, even though we may not necessarily have the approval of people. You do what is within the realm of possibilities for you and God will do the impossible!

16

THE MOST FAMOUS WEDDING IN HISTORY

So, what does another wedding have to do with this story, the reader may ask. The celebration of this extraordinary wedding and the events that follow will have such a significant impact that it will affect all nations, as well as past, present and future generations. In other words, the most famous wedding in history will have an impact for all eternity!

Though every person receives an invitation to participate in this wedding –yes, including you, perhaps many times throughout your life – ot everyone responds affirmatively. The reason is that some people will be distracted, others will be involved in multiple activities or excitedly purchasing everything the world has to offer; while others will be shedding tears of sorrow, or weariness of their journey and will not have energy to do anything more. Ultimately, many people will not give priority to attending such an event in their life, because they do not comprehend the importance and impact that this event will have in history.

Does it seem strange that a wedding could affect you and even change the course of history? At one time, I also thought it was strange. Nevertheless, during my journey in search of genuine and unconditional love, capable of filling the depths of my soul, I began to discover that this story is real. Truly the most significant element I have found in my life is the genuine and unconditional love of God. Next I'll share with you how I came to accept the invitation to participate in this phenomenal wedding ceremony, which you will not want to miss.

A famous love story

In literature there are many famous love stories. Romeo and Juliet are one of the most unforgettable couples in literary history. From a seemingly endless brawl between two families, a feeling of love at first sight flourishes between two of these family members. Unaware that they belong to rival families, a strong attraction between the young Romeo and enchanting Juliet emerges during a party, after they exchange dialogue and a kiss. From that moment on, they are in a love trance. When the youths find out each other's identity, they feel disheartened because they have lost hope in the possibility of reconciliation for their families, after such a long history of hate and resentment. In spite of this situation they each vow eternal love for each other.

Later, Lawrence, a priest, and Romeo's confessor –though surprised to know the youths are in love– agrees to secretly marry the lovers in hope of ending the prolonged animosity between the Capulet and Montague families. When Juliet's father finds out about his daughter's affection toward Romeo, he plans to marry her with another man, so she will relinquish her affections towards Romeo. However, the minister marries the couple and ingeniously plans to help them escape to avoid the other wedding. According to the plan, Juliet would take a potion that would temporarily put her to sleep while her friends flee with her body. Sadly, Romeo only hears that Juliet has died, because the messenger that was going to explain that Juliet was only asleep never arrives with the news.

Juliet's family finds her and believing her to be dead; they weep and place her on top of the tomb. When Romeo arrives, believing that Juliet has died, he decides to take his life rather than live without her. He buys poison to finalize his existence and hurriedly goes to Juliet's tomb.

There, he finds Paris –the other man whom her family wanted her to marry– they fight and Romeo kills him. When Romeo observes Juliet's inert body, he drinks the poison and dies beside her. Later, Juliet awakens to see her beloved and realizing what has happened, she kisses him in hopes that the venom from his lips will also poison her. When that does not occur, she takes Romeo's knife and stabs herself in the chest, falling down upon Romeo's body.

Finally, the keeper, the prince and members of the Capulet and Montague families are together at the tomb with the bodies. The scene is so moving, that the families decide to terminate their longstanding feud and in honor of their children's love, erect golden statues, side by side. From that day on, the city of Veron becomes a peaceful place.

The human heart vibrates with these stories because they represent the possibility that we too may find that special someone who will wholeheartedly accept, value and care for us; in other words, someone that truly loves us. This is one reason why people are fascinated with soap operas that transport viewers to an illusion where they can indirectly live the character's story. It is not difficult to consider –for a detailed observer– that the majority of viewers dedicated to novels, desire that state of "being in love" and the feelings of unity and understanding that those stories represent. Perhaps, if the audiences of novels such as these had a good relationship with their partners, they would invest more time with them, rather than in front of the screen engrossed in those daily, unending fantasies. Many people either don't have a partner, or those who do often do not share good dialogue or have a loving, committed, deep and satisfying relationship. The fact there is such a market and attachment to this literary genre strongly attests to this possibility.

The royal wedding of 2011

Why is it that people feel so much attraction for love? Love is the theme most written about, the inspiration of most musical compositions and as a fact, the most powerful feeling and force in the universe. A love story touches the intimate fibers and longing within us. It enchants our imagination because it embraces our hope and dream, even if latently of achieving this reality. Ultimately, it is the dream of happiness. The ideal of happiness attracts both young and old alike, as the world proved with the wedding of Prince William, Duke of Cambridge, –second in line to inherit the British throne– and Catherine Middleton, Duchess of Cambridge in Westminster Abbey. Approximately two and a half million people around the world synchronized their attention on April 29, 2011, whether in person, through television screens or the Internet, to witness this royal wedding. Queen Elizabeth II and Prince Philip, grandparents of the groom, his father Charles, and stepmother, his many kinsman, friends, and acquaintances, distinguished aristocrats from other countries, heads of State, actors and singers and a parade of famous people were among the 1,900 guests who came together to celebrate this event. Eyewitnesses and media spectators looked on, absorbed by the beauty, colors, fashions, extravagant hats, street adornments, military parades, diversity of luxurious automobiles, horse-driven carriages dressed in the same colors, exquisite food, not to mention the music that filled the air in different ambiances. There was not a respectable news agency lacking presence in the Westminster Abbey ceremony or in the reception that followed at the Buckingham palace.

Every culture in the world, in one way or another, celebrates a wedding –or its equivalent– with the best they have and can purchase. The happiness spreads to the entire family and friends of bride and groom. For some cultures the wedding lasts hours, while others celebrate them over the course of days or weeks. This type of celebration is a special time to forget sorrows, difficulties, illness and wars to concentrate on the joyful, beautiful and positive aspects that life offers. A wedding also ensures we will be remembered through our children and grandchildren, who will carry on the family name. It is the possibility of a strong union between spouses, greater material wealth and the extension of grandparent's and parent's lives, by achieving through their children and grandchildren what perhaps they were not able to accomplish. Ultimately, the children to come are the hope of the future, for whom we work and to whom we bequeath all the effort of our experience and labor.

At the same time, those who do not celebrate a wedding tend to be those who are unknown by or distant from the celebrating family and therefore do not receive an invitation; and those who openly disagree with the union of the couple. Often, those who know the couple yet are not invited feel excluded, disregarded and often insulted. By contrast, those who are invited to a great ceremony enhance not just their social status within the group to which they belong, but their self-esteem increases. The more renowned or important the bride, groom and their family are, the higher the category bequeathed the guests. Most certainly, if you would have received an invitation to participate in Princess Catherine and Prince William's wedding you probably would have accepted to participate if you were able. Why not?

An invitation to the greatest ceremony

In my case, since I was a child, I longed to find that profound love and get married. I wanted to find a perfect love and come to the altar with a white dress on my wedding day. However, with time I understood that no one can love us unconditionally, even if they wanted to, simply because as human beings we do not have the capacity to love in this way! After so much stumbling, I finally understood this and my perspective changed. I realized that unconditional love could come only from the one that can love us unconditionally, God! Now, I would like to share some insights about this incomparable love of God and what we can do to experience it personally.

It all started with the acceptance of an invitation. This invitation gives me entrance to the most famous wedding in history, for which I have been preparing. I will attend this ceremony, along with millions of other people. These invitations have been distributed throughout time, in every century and throughout the utmost corners of the world. Carefully chosen people have handed out these invitations in towns and major cities. In remote mountainous areas and warm breeze coastal regions, the carriers have delivered, because as messengers they comprehended the unique impact that this celebration will have.

Some of the messengers went to villages, while others with extensive connections spread the word of this event through various media including radio, the press, television, and Internet, including social media such as Twitter and Facebook. They announced that all people were invited. Those sent covered the earth with the message of the greatest, deepest, most sincere and complete love story that has ever been experienced. All people are invited; nevertheless, many will exclude themselves by simply not accepting the invitation!

The celebration to which I will attend is based on a covenant; an unconditional love promise which implies commitment and loyalty that lasts forever. It is not the type of love that many promise but that only lasts until the money runs out or until another person crosses their path who is either more attractive, interesting, has a better position, is younger, has less pounds or wants to take on the position without titles or commitments.

Never before has this type of wedding been witnessed. It marks the beginning of a new era in the history of humanity with a union that will establish perpetual peace among all the peoples and kingdoms of the earth. However, for there to be long-lasting peace, truth and justice must necessarily be in the equation. At the time of this wedding, a new social order with different conditions will arise thus ending pain, weeping, wickedness and death. In addition, the worst of human sentiments will be vanished: ignorance, self-centeredness, pride, fear and deception.

The day of the long awaited and spectacular wedding has arrived!

What joy is seen in the bride and groom, their families and friends because the long awaited day is here, the celebration of the great wedding feast[1]. Those who have found each other and strived for their love are finally uniting as one. This is the day millions of people from every nation, tongue, and tribe have longed for[2]. A great multitude, whose number cannot be counted[3], will participate in the most important ceremony of history! Many, many were invited, but few, in comparison, were chosen to participate[4].

The hosts have prepared every detail, and everything is now ready. The bride had announced that everyone could come freely and join them on this great day[5]. However, those who will be able to attend the celebration are those who accepted, confirmed, and prepared themselves for it. It is those who prepared themselves and have their names written in the guest book. Blessed are those who are able to participate in the great wedding banquet[6].

So who are the bride and groom? Why is this wedding so important? Why is it significant for you? I will share how the couple was engaged and the impact that their union has for you and for humanity.

The bride had been a flirtatious girl, described also as a sexually unrestrained woman from her youth. She had many admirers and lovers and she took advantage of each one. Yet she had a special admirer whom she really paid no attention to. She despised his attentions, words, and gestures of love. In spite of this, he continued to seek her, offering his genuine love. With patience and devotion he persisted although she remained reluctant pursuing her many lovers.

However, he looked not only at her current condition, but had the capacity to perceive the young girl's phenomenal potential; he saw her capacity to learn, to grow and the abilities she had to give to the world. Although she was beautiful, her physical beauty was not her greatest attraction for the young man. He looked deeper and observed her internal beauty. He saw what others didn't even care to contemplate, or think of. This young man loved her with a deep and true love. He could have gotten tired and given up after so many insults and rejections; nevertheless, the unrelenting young man persisted in quest of her when she fled and cohabitated with her lovers.

The young man knew he could conquer her heart, because love wins! The others did not truly love her; they only used her to satisfy their momentary pleasure. He loved her truly and infallibly and he demonstrated it. When he found her sad, he consoled her soul with words that filled her with life; if he found her wounded, he cured her, if she was sick, he healed her. When she was impoverished, he supplied her needs. Nonetheless, she arrogantly and ruthlessly forgot the many manifestations of his genuine love. She pretended to be doing well, extremely confident in her many charms and diverse lovers. That's why time after time she resisted the young man's romantic intentions. Even so, he believed he could triumph if she gave him a sincere opportunity.

Time moved forward and she began to realize the quality of love that this young man offered and the authenticity of that love. He was a gentleman in every way. He cared for her tenderly and brought her fine gifts. His conduct was beyond reproach and his actions began to conquer her distrustful and discouraged heart. With his strength of character, sweetness and words he gave her hope, joy and life.

Somehow, she thought it was too late. She had sold herself to that licentious lifestyle and felt she could not be free from it. One day, she finally reflected, "of what good are these lovers who don't value me? They lie and take advantage of my weaknesses. Yet on the other hand, he is willing to give his life for me. What have I done to deserve his respect and love? What does he see in me? In spite of how badly I have behaved, and even after I sold myself in slavery, he continues to patiently forgive and seek me with his unwavering affection, not requesting anything in exchange."

The young man not only wins her heart but he ultimately buys her from that lifestyle, paying a high price for her. Even though the girl feels unworthy and guilty, with so many demonstrations of pure love she decides to accept the invitation that he offers to be free from slavery and become his fiancé, bride and future wife.

The distinguished gentleman invites her to follow him to his father's land. Then he shares with her about the customs of his land where he would go to prepare a home for her[7]. He would then return for her and meanwhile she too would prepare. Her challenge would be to learn another language, a new way of life and laws and even a different way of dressing and eating. She was not sure if she wanted to change everything she knew for the unknown, since it was difficult for her to believe what she was hearing. With so much betrayal and infidelity in the culture that she knew, it seemed impossible to find a person of integrity in whom to trust.

However, no one spoke as he did; so sure of what he affirmed, like one who knows and has experience. Besides, what he promised, he fulfilled, and his words were true, backed up by the ultimate authority, time and facts which confirmed the words of this man. Finally, she felt that her appreciation had turned into love, and her love into devotion. The young man conquered her heart, not with manipulations and deceit, but with the strength of truth, the power of his convictions and a prevailing pure love.

In his arms, she felt secure, coupled with an indescribable peace and joy. She then wanted to please her fiancé, thus corresponding to his level of surrender and commitment. At last she was unconditionally loved, respected, valued and protected. Every person longs for this type of relationship –yes, this is also true for men spiritually– in the deepest part of their being; and at last, she had found it! Besides, he had freed her from slavery, from the exploitation of her lovers, from her gloomy past and from the pain that she had brought on herself by her own mistaken decisions.

Then came a deliberate and rigorous stage of preparation. She needed to relearn several routines, change her habits and her destructive way of living. She became disciplined and learned a new language, read about the traditions of the Kingdom where she would live. She comprehended that the different way of living gave her peace and inner strength, thus she finally decided to eradicate from her soul the attraction for her former lovers and empty customs. Initially, she thought she would not succeed. She struggled with her character and feelings. However, her fiancé offered all of the necessary support. Besides he left her a spectacular helper so that she could overcome. She also wanted to get in shape and look her best for the wedding day; so she began to prepare physically, mentally and spiritually for the changes that would come.

Incomparable!

After a while, her fiancé came back for her, according to his promise, and he took her to his father's land, where he had prepared their dwelling. From then on, they would never be apart and no one could take away the joy of their union[8]. The bride was ready[9]. She had prepared herself in many ways and was wearing her white gown made of shining white linen that her fiancé had purchased at a high price. She had not paid for it because she could not afford it, yet she would wear it with honor and from that day forward she would live to join all her efforts and desires with her future husband. In addition, she had willingly sought instruction and learned to perform just and compassionate acts for those who needed them, like her fiancé desired. The fine linen represented those righteous acts[10]. She felt joyous giving her time and talent to help others, and because of this she now stood out among women. The bride had also prepared herself by anointing her face and hair with fragrant aromas that were attractive to the senses[11].

The guests of honor were also ready, those who were willing to pay a high price for this wedding to occur. All of them dressed for the occasion, with white clothes whiter than any earthly manufacturer can make them[12]. The white clothes represented the righteousness of those who wore them[13]. The splendor represented physical health as well as emotional health and above all, a vigorous spiritual life. This health was manifested in harmony with their Creator, with themselves, with others and with the natural environment in which they lived.

The long awaited wedding celebration began. For a few seconds, she remembered the many obstacles she had to overcome until this day. Now she knew all the pain and suffering had been worthwhile, since she had attained the maximum victory and was actually now in a place of honor. Her fears, uncertainty and pain were behind her. She would now see her fiancé, who after much toil and suffering had conquered her unfaithful heart, having given everything for her.

The choir sounded like angelic beings singing while the musicians played beautiful harmonies. There was no need for lights because the splendor of her Father-in-law's light filled every corner of the place[14]. The bride was joyous. The door to the chapel opened and the aroma of fresh flowers flooded the sanctuary. She stood at the entrance, where the maids of honor began to walk toward the altar. She breathed deeply and advanced among the guests, who were all standing on either side, listening to the wedding march.

However, at that very instant she realized... Just then she understood who her beloved was! He had a crown on his head and his countenance radiated with light. His name was Prince of Peace, King of kings and Lord of lords[15 & 16]. Then she understood that He had been given all authority, power and dominion in heaven and on earth[17]. She understood that she had been created for that time. What eye has not seen and ear has not heard and has not entered into the heart of man, God has prepared for those who love Him[18].

The ceremony was splendorous! The Prince and his bride declared their pact of eternal love. All of her past was now behind her and she was flooded with the greatest sensation of joy she had ever experienced. All sorrow had vanished and the pain, contempt, anguish, fear, rejection and tribulation she had previously experienced seemed to be only a distant nightmare.

The guests looked at her marveled to see that now she was crowned with glory. The one who had previously been deserted and helpless, embarrassed and desolate was now married and protected, and her husband's Father was exceedingly glad[19]. Her husband wiped all tears from her eyes and she would never again cry over her sorrows[20]. Not her, nor any of the guests, will ever again experience the effects of death, or illness[21]. In this place, there will be no more pain, war or destruction[22]. There will also be no more vengeance, shame, selfishness or curse[23]. Her joy was a perpetual joy, because they were now in the Kingdom of Peace[24] from where they would never have to leave.

As a result of this union, every human being will live in a new social order, not under human governments that are corrupt and serve their own interests; nor with other selfish beings eager to violate each other's rights or other hateful feelings characteristic of the kingdoms of the earth. Death will no longer reign. This union meant the beginning of a new era of pure consciousness, in which everyone will know themselves transparently, without masks, or lies. Peace and harmony will reign there and the desire to build up together in unity. Every person will have the capacity to develop their potential and the opportunity to love and be loved legitimately and honestly. Who, in the bottom of their heart would not like to live like this? Honestly, I do not think there is a person who would prefer to live like we live on earth today.

After the ceremony, all those who had come from the East, West, North and South also went to the banquet and sat at the table[25]. Blessed are those who are permitted to sit and eat at this extraordinary table[26].

Those who did not attend this grand ceremony were the ones that excluded themselves by not accepting the invitation, by not preparing themselves[27] or reserving their seat in the guest book that allowed them to enter[28].

Have you accepted this invitation? Make your reservation today to attend this wedding and the banquet and afterwards be able to participate in a glorious new life.

The interpretation of this narration

The story I have just described is not a fairy tale. It is a vision of the near future, backed up by Jesus Christ whose irreproachable life, along with his words and deeds affirmed it. Until now, all of the prophesies in the book to which he continuously referred –the Bible– have come to pass exactly as it was foretold throughout history. Why would the last few prophesies not follow the same pattern?

For clarification of those who are not familiar with the Biblical text, Jesus is the groom and the bride consists of the group of people or followers of Christ, who have believed that he was crucified for them to give them eternal life and to show them a new and better way of living. These followers believe that Jesus, unlike any other person who has ever lived, rose from the dead and is alive today. Though the first time he came as a helpless baby, he will return as absolute King of this earth. The Heavenly Father is preparing and perfecting, maturing and sanctifying every person committed to Christ, who forms a body called the church, in order to present her as a gift to the Lord Jesus Christ, who will marry her, forever. If you would like to learn more about the biblical prophesies that have been fulfilled and other detailed information on many other aspects of Christianity, you can read the book: New evidence that Demands a Verdict, by Josh MacDowell.

This story is the greatest love story that any person has ever known. Human love, including maternal love, which is the love that most closely resembles the love of God, is imperfect and frequently conditional. It becomes weary, gives up and changes, because we either voluntarily kill it, others kill it in us, or because human beings die. Besides, the person who loves is almost always looking for something in return, even if only to be acknowledged. Although God desires our love, He loves us even when we hate him or when we do not recognize how deep the love he has for us as a father is. So you must be asking yourself, how can you love God? What words does God himself use to describe to us His great love? Since his love is perfect, we could learn much from him.

The best known description of God's unconditional love is in the book of the Bible known as the First Letter from Paul to the Corinthians. It is the first of two books written to the church in the city of Corinth. Chapter 13 expresses the unrelenting love of God. Read it carefully and you will see the depth of God's love, which is the measure of love he offers you and me.

My Paraphrased version

1 If I spoke various languages, both human and of angels, yet do not know how to love, I am only like metal pieces making noise.

2 If I knew the future, and understood all the mysteries of science, and if I had faith so great as to achieve miracles, including moving mountains from place to another, and do not have love, I am nothing.

3 If I gave away all of my material possessions to feed the needy, and even donated my body as an offering to be burnt for others, and do not know how to love, it would be useless.

4 Love knows how to withstand suffering, it has no ill intentions, no envy of others, and does not covet the possessions, positions or relationships of other people; it does not speak much about itself, nor does it think higher of him or herself than others.

5 Love never does anything that can hurt or damage another person, it does not seek its own advantage, nor is it impatient; it does not keep score of offenses because it knows how to forgive.

6 It is not happy when unjust or evil situations occur to others, but it is joyful when truth comes to light and justice is executed.

7 True love suffers all, believes all, hopes for all and withstands all.

8 He who loves never stops loving. Yet predictions about the future will one day terminate, and speaking in many languages will also stop as will science come to its end.

9 Because we know some things and others we predict.

10 Yet when He who is perfect reveals himself, then the imperfections will exist no more.

11 When I was young, my thoughts and words were those of a child, I did not have the capacity of understanding, or judging with the depth of an adult; yet when I grew up, I left behind what was immature.

12 Now we see only uncertain reflections because there is little light; however, in the future we will see closely, and in full daylight. Now I know some of reality, but in the future I will understand with the level of truth, detail and depth with which God has known me.

13 Now three feelings endure above all others, faith, hope and love. However, the one that surpasses them all in excellence is love. These three remain, faith, hope and love, yet of the three the greatest is love (I Corinthians 13).

The most outstanding of all is love

Only God has the depth of love, described in I Corinthians, for each human being He created. There you are among them in this equation. The Bible narrates the many attempts God has made to reveal himself to you, to show you who He is and His desire to transform your reality. God's heart is in pain when he sees our pain and he has a plan to change the course, not just of our personal history, but of the history of humanity, towards a future of lasting peace and joy.

You may compare the following portions of Scripture (the Bible) to better understand the complete message they contain. Although deep, it is simple enough for a child to understand. When John, the youngest of Jesus' disciples had become an old man, he had a tremendously complex vision. God showed him the future and several of the events that would occur. John narrates his encounter as follows, "The angel told me, write, 'Blessed are those called to the wedding of the Lamb.'" In addition, he said, "These are true words from God"[29]. Read for yourself some of the portions that explain in more detail the invitation to the coming great wedding.

The bridegroom, Jesus, is the first to invite you to participate in the wedding. "So he sent other servants to tell them, 'The feast has been prepared. The bulls and fattened cattle have been killed, and everything is ready. Come to the banquet!"[30] Jesus invites all of humanity to participate. He does not reject anyone. However, "The time has come," he said, "The kingdom of God has come near. Repent and believe the good news!"[31] To receive the invitation to the wedding, we must recognize our offenses towards others and our rebellion against God. Our own merits cannot purchase or gain for us God's forgiveness. We need Christ who offered the perfect sacrifice. No one else has lived a holy life, in perfect communion with God the Father and with those that surrounded him. For this reason, not even those they call prophets or saints can grant us salvation. Jesus responded, the Son of Man must be lifted up, so that everyone who believes in him will have eternal life![32]

Jesus replied, "I tell you the truth, unless you are born again you cannot see the Kingdom of God[33]. In other words, it is only through personal commitment that all who believe in Him won't perish, but have eternal life. To receive this gift you require the simplicity of a child.

"I tell you the truth, anyone who doesn't receive the Kingdom of God like a child will never enter it"[34]. Adults tend to be proud, and to harden their heart, as well as to over rationalize. A child is sincere, open and trusting. You also need to believe that Jesus came, died for us and rose from the dead to show us a new way to live. Simply receive His gift of salvation.

Likewise, those who have set their hope on the material things of this world, or in themselves, will with much difficulty recognize their need of God. "How hard it is for the rich to enter the Kingdom of God!"[35] Jesus taught that most of all people need spiritual poverty so that money does not become the security of their life. Jesus said, "Blessed are the poor, for the Kingdom of God is yours"[36]. Only Christ is capable of restoring our relationship with God the Father.

"John the Baptist saw Jesus coming toward him and said, 'Look! The Lamb of God who takes away the sin of the world!'"[37] "It was the precious blood of Christ, the sinless, spotless Lamb of God. God chose him as your ransom long before the world began, but he has now revealed him to you in these last days.[38] Through Christ you have come to trust in God, and you have placed your faith and hope in God because he raised Christ from the dead and gave him great glory"[39]. "Jesus told him, 'I am the way, the truth and the life. No one can come to the Father except through me"[40]. We start as being God's creation or creatures, and become God's children when we understand and obey His truths. Then the Spirit of God works an incredible transformation in us and also renews our interpersonal relationships, through non-deceitful fraternal love. God teaches us to love one another wholeheartedly and with a pure heart. Here Jesus declares that to love God necessarily implies and manifests itself in loving our neighbor and serving him, because when someone who is a stranger is hungry and thirsty, naked, sick or alone; whatever we do with that person is what we are indirectly doing with God[41].

Those who accept the invitation will receive the necessary power to triumph, because they will start to learn to not depend solely on their own strength, but on the strength that comes from the Holy Spirit. One day the Pharisees asked Jesus, 'When will the Kingdom of God come?' He replied, "The Kingdom of God can't be detected by visible signs. You won't be able to say, 'Here it is!' or 'It's over there!' For the Kingdom of God is already among you"[41]. Are you seeking God? You may not have realized how close he is to you, and how willing he is to hear you, transform you and give you abundant life.

"Then one of the seven angels who held the seven bowls containing the seven last plagues came and said to me, 'Come with me! I will show you the bride, the wife of the Lamb[42] in other words, those that live in the great city." For those not familiar with Biblical terminology, the marriage relationship represents or appears as a symbol of the relationship between Christ and his people, the church[43].

"But now the Good News of the Kingdom of God is preached, and everyone is eager to get in. But that doesn't mean that the law has lost its force. It is easier for heaven and earth to disappear than for the smallest point of God's law (The Bible) to be overturned"[44].

I ask you dear reader; do you think it is important to participate in the celebration I have described? Can you capture the great vision that God has to transform the entire mess that we, human beings, have created and to change our course toward what is real and will bring lasting peace and joy for all?

He, Jesus, invites you. Millions upon millions of people that follow him wholeheartedly invite you, and I invite you. Only your Creator loves you unconditionally. Accept His invitation to participate in this ceremony that you will not want to miss. Simply surrender the reins of your life to God. Recognize how much harm you have done to others and to yourself by living without divine principles as the guide for your decisions and actions. Leave your pride and arrogance aside that causes you to believe you can do anything on your own. When you are sincere with yourself and come before Him without false pretense, He will prepare your heart and mind to a new and marvelous way of living (amplified Bible).

Try it and see for yourself. You have nothing to lose! On the contrary, you have everything to gain!

The Amplified Bible says, "The [Holy] Spirit and the bride (the church, the true Christians) say, Come! And let him who is listening say, Come! And let everyone come who is thirsty [who is painfully conscious of his need of those things by which the soul is refreshed, supported, and strengthened]; and whoever [earnestly] desires to do it, let him come, take, appropriate, and drink the water of Life without cost"[45].

IMMIGRATION ISSUES WITH HISPANICS IN THE USA

The immigration situation is a controversial one within many circles in the The immigration situation is a controversial one within many circles in the United States today. Because of this, I did not want to ignore this relevant portion of my story and the manner by which my family and I arrived in this country. Although I do not expect to exhaust all of the elements of this issue in a few paragraphs, I do believe it is important to mention critical data and key aspects of this reflection. I bring up the topic to educate us Latinos and understand with greater clarity why many North Americans feel irritated with the illegal population in their country. On the other hand, it is quite sad that having arrived at the land of opportunity, so many Hispanics have not taken advantage of the many resources available to help them succeed. Statistics show that many Hispanics that come to live in the United States continue to be submerged in poverty, living In ignorance and in the same patterns of negative social behavior that kept them in bondage in their own countries. It's time to question these social patterns. I don't necessarily question the beautiful, admirable and healthy customs our people have, yet I do question those social habits that blind, sink, and destroy. It is time to change, people.

The United States is indisputably, a nation of immigrants from all corners of the earth. Immigrants have enriched this country with their array of thought, talent and energy. Diversity has been an enormous strength and pillar of what this nation has become today. Many immigrants have successfully obtained high ranks of distinction and leadership, standing out in different positions of society such as, business, education, science, sports, medicine and government.

However, there are other causes of concern, such as the statistics from the Pew Hispanic Center, which is well known for its research[46]. For example, studies carried out by the center affirm that although Latino youths between 16-25 years of age say they feel optimistic and satisfied with their lives and possible future and that they value education and work, as well as success in their careers of tomorrow. However, reality demonstrates that it is more likely that children of Hispanic descent will abandon their secondary education and become adolescent parents.

In conclusion, Hispanics, more than other races such as whites and Asians, tend to live in poverty. Two-thirds of surveyed youths, who are descendants from Latino immigrants, struggle between two cultures. The Pew Hispanic Center asks questions such as, what are the values, experiences, attitudes and identity of the generation of Hispanic descendents in the United States once they reach adulthood. This is one of the key questions that we, Latino adults, should also be formulating ourselves. The fact is that this has to do with our children[47]. Don't you think it is worrisome?

Statistics about Latinos in the United States, based on the National Census of 2010

Detailed reports summarize results based on the analysis and impact that the illegal population has on social services and programs funded by the government such as, education, health care, application and maintenance of law and justice, as well as other public assistance programs.

By the 2010 census date in the United States, during the previous 10 years the Hispanic population grew by 46.3%. This growth went from 35.3 million to 50.5 million, reaching 6.3% of the global US population by 2011.

In March of 2010, experts calculated that there were approximately 11.2 million illegal immigrants living the United States. Although the Mexican population makes up the largest group of illegal immigrants in the country, the truth is that immigration from Mexico significantly declined between 2000-2010. The Pew Center states that the entrance of illegal people has reduced especially in the Southwestern mountainous zones of the nation due in part to increased border patrolling.

The largest three groups of Hispanic origin are Mexicans, Puerto Ricans and Cubans. The four subgroups that follow, which have grown most during the last decade were, Salvadorians, Dominicans, Guatemalans and Colombians. In spite of their status as the dominant group, Mexicans are not the largest Hispanic group in all of the country's metropolitan areas. For example, Cubans are the predominant group in Miami. In the Washington D.C. area Salvadorians hold that distinction, while in the New York / New Jersey area it is Puerto Ricans. The largest group of Hispanic origin in metropolitan cities such as Los Angeles-Long Beach, Chicago and San Antonio are Mexicans[48].

Another interesting fact is that the Mexican-American population grew by 7.2 million from new births compared to an increase of only 4.3 million from non-authorized or illegal immigrants. The birth rate among Latino women is greater than that of other races[49].

During the 1990s, the number of undocumented people doubled every year. It is estimated that 13 million foreigners, both legal as well as non-documented, made the US their permanent residence.

Alarming statistics on criminology[50]

Initially, let us clarify that the information below is not an affirmation against Hispanic immigrants. These are more facts concerning Illegal aliens, in general, who come from all nationalities and backgrounds. Annually, some 72,000 foreigners are incarcerated for offenses related to drugs and statistics show that 25% of the federal jail population is illegal. This means that less than 5% of the population commits 25% of the crimes.

Ninety-five percent of homicide arrest warrants in Los Angeles alone, approximately 1,500 yearly, are committed by illegal aliens. In addition, of the 17,000 pending fugitive felony warrants 67% belong to illegal aliens. In Lake County, Illinois, half of murder crimes and 21.5% of those behind bars are illegal and cost the county in one year $4,056,945 dollars. During the 1999 fiscal year the cost to taxpayers in Pennsylvania for incarcerating undocumented people increased to $133 million. It is estimated that the annual national cost to maintain illegal criminals is over two billion. Of some 400,000 undocumented people that have committed a crime, and have been issued a deportation warrant, a great majority have fled from the law and their whereabouts are unknown.

2011 Report concerning fiscal costs to tax payers for illegal immigration in the USA.

The greatest cost is in educating the children of people who are illegal. With an annual cost of almost $52 billion, these costs are absorbed by State and Local Governments. The main cause for the cost is because the great majority of illegal aliens do not pay taxes on their income. Of those that do pay income tax, many request tax credits resulting in payments that the government must reimburse, thus diminishing income collected to provide free services. Overall, expenses related to illegal immigration costs taxpayers some $113 mil million annually (2011). At the Federal, State and Local levels these costs must be absorbed without the possibility of collecting the corresponding income from those that use all of these social services[51].

Concerns that US residents and citizens have

For non-Hispanic populations, the most significant concerns regarding illegal immigrants are not just the high costs that illegal families generate in all types of services, such as education, health care, and legal assistance. There is another facet that is well documented, and it is the criminal activity that stems from the Hispanic population

I am not advocating whether a new amnesty program would be favorable or not. I just want to highlight that many of the problems that our Latino community faces today has to do precisely with the same issues and difficulties that I have narrated in my own history. For those of us that now live in the United States, it is not the lack of opportunities in education or work. Instead, the majority of Latinos continue making decisions that do not favor family life, among them irresponsible fatherhood, the failure to not finish our secondary education and even continue on to higher education when there are so many scholarships, and excellent educational centers and universities. The lack of a well-balanced and nutritional diet, domestic abuse, both physically and psychologically, and the exploitation rooted in chauvinism in so many homes produces these social ailments that generate children with many internal conflicts. If we are not willing to recognize it and take action, our cultural heritage will not change, nor will the future of our children even though we now live in a world power.

Brief historical background

Illegal immigration seriously captivated US government attention as early as 1875 when they issued a federal law prohibiting the entrance into the country of convicts and prostitutes. President Chester A. Arthur also prohibited beggars and those with mental illnesses to enter the country. Up to that time, the distinction between legal and illegal immigrants did not exist.

The strongest wave, or influx of immigration was from 1881 to 1920 when some 23 million people came to the US from from all parts of the world. In order to ensure the country's ethnical composition and be able to assimilate the 15 million immigrants from South and East Europe –who had immigrated during the previous 40 years– Congress passed quotas limiting immigration. These quotas were for 1921, 1924 and 1929 based on acceptance by country of origin.

Nevertheless, the doors for Mexico and Northern European countries remained open, because employers saw the convenience of cheap hand labor. This open door was what, with time became non authorized immigration.

In 1928, the Senate Committee for Immigration highlighted the fiscal weight caused by the non restricted influx of Mexicans on tax contributors in regards to hospital services, prison expenses and other social services. They estimated that while 67,000 Mexicans entered legally, thousands more were entering illegally.

During the great depression and market crash of 1929, the US seriously restricted its immigration laws with Mexico. Due to possible deportations and employment scarcity, approximately one million Mexicans abandoned the country. However, during World War II, because of insufficient hand labor the US government designed a plan, known as Programa Bracero to attract temporary agricultural laborers for the southwestern portion of the country.

Initially, it was expected that these laborers would come during the harvest times and then return to their countries; thus for the next two decades, some 4.8 million Mexican laborers came to provide their cheap labor to employers. The program ended in 1964, after unions complained that these workers were taking jobs away from legal residents. The Los Angeles Times declared in May, 1950, that the border with Mexico was flooded by an infinite and unprecedented wave in national history of people who were crossing the border.

The government calculated that during Dwight D. Eisenhower's first term in office, illegal immigrants crossing at different points of the border exceeded one million people, generating a massive labor force that had an impact on North American workers and caused a new and corrupt market based on illegal hand laborers.

In 1954, President Eisenhower named General Joseph Swing as the head of the Immigration who announced the start of Operation Wetback. This measure sparked a deportation of thousands of non-authorized immigrants, while at the same time thousands more returned to their countries of origin. By the end of the 1950s, illegal immigration had decreased by 95%. However, the trend did not last long and in 1963, the Immigration Act opened the border. Then, along with legal immigration, illegal immigration grew rapidly, to the point that to this day, the primary source of legal and illegal immigration comes from Mexico.

Likewise, the incentive to obtain "birthright citizenship" has motivated many hopefuls to remain in the United States, knowing that the probabilities of their being deported will be lessened if they have an offspring who is an American citizen, who, by the way, can also qualify to receive benefits and services financed by the state. When analyzing this long and controversial reality, Congress has passed seven amnesties since 1965, starting with the "Immigration and Nationality Act."

First, 1986: The Immigration and Reform Control Act (IRCA), encompassed some three million illegal aliens. This was the largest of the reforms in which unfortunately, much fraud occurred with the documentation. Additionally, the numbers who came forward far surpassed the expectations for which the act was designed. For these reasons, the law was considered a failure, and there was no political will to enforce the law against employers of illegal immigrants.

Second, 1994: Section 245(i) Amnesty, was rolling or inclusive in nature and was granted to 578,000.

Third, 1997: Section 245(i) Extension Amnesty, was an extension of the existing 1994 law.

Fourth, 1997: Nicaraguan Adjustment and Central American Relief Act (NACARA) Amnesty, made provision for upwards of one million non-authorized people from Nicaragua and Central America to become legal.

Fifth, 1998: Haitian Refugee Immigration Fairness Act Amnesty (HRIFA), was approved for 125,000 non documented Haitians.

Sixth, 2000: Late Amnesty, included people who protested saying they should have been included under the previous 1986 and authorized residency for another 400,000 people.

Seventh, 2000: LIFE Act Amnesty Section 245(i), reactivated the rolling amnesty with which another 900,000 people became legal residents.

Although President Bill Clinton made efforts to combat illegal immigration, the situation remained more or less unchanged. Thus, when the Illegal Immigration Reform and Immigrant Responsibility Act, of 1996 passed, there were some 7 million illegal immigrants.

During George W. Bush's administration, the enforcement of immigration laws became lax again, and it was no surprise that in 2005, there were an estimated 10-20 million illegal immigrants in the country.

In 2007, the Washington Post affirmed that nearly 6 million businesses employed more than 7 million illegal workers. Today, more than 1 million immigrants enter the Unites States legally every year, while the illegal population grows at the rate of approximately 500,000 annually. The majority of people enter via Mexico, including people from other Central American countries. Only 6% of illegal immigrants arrive from Canada or Europe. Almost half of the people entering the US arrive legally; however, they become illegal by extending their stay beyond the authorized time period stated on their visas.

Historically, the federal government has failed to secure the borders, and adequately monitor those with temporary visas. Of the non-authorized population, estimated in 2011 to be between 15-20 million, the greatest number of these, some 2.4 million people, resides in California. Other states with large illegal populations are Texas, Florida and New York. [52 & 53].

As mentioned earlier, among the greatest concerns regarding the situation of illegal immigrants is the economic impact on all of the services, including schools and hospitals which are already overpopulated. It is also impossible to omit the noticeable increase in crime. The government estimates that in California alone, since 2004, the net costs for taxpayers annually to provide services for undocumented immigrants is nine billion.

On one side of the debate, those who are in favor of legalizing all illegal people say that since we cannot round up and deport 12 million people, then we must provide a road to legality, with a path towards future citizenship. In spite of the opposition to this measure, there are groups that are pressuring President Obama to authorize another amnesty.

In any event, one thing is certain. Many people from Latin American countries that immigrated to the United States are–as my friend and economist Jaime

Malone says– "economic refugees". Therefore, authorities need to implement humane measures that follow common sense, with a feasible cost benefit for those involved. As some people have proposed already, temporary legal venues for people who wish to work in the US for a specific time frame could be a viable solution, providing it is authorized and audited.

Now that you have more precise information, think about it, what do you now think about the situation of illegal immigrants in this country? In the first decade of the 21st century, Hispanic Americans have become the fastest growing minority in the United States. Experts are predicting this trend to continue, until at least 2015. It is important to observe from the data extracted during the last census that in comparison with the rest of the population, the average age of Hispanics is 27.7 years, versus 36.8 for the rest of the population. In addition, 34% of Hispanics are younger than 18, compared to 25% of the rest of the population. According to the 2010 Census, by the year 2050 people of Hispanic descent will make up 25% of the total population in the nation. This scenario has significant implications for the economy, the country's culture, the labor market and other areas.

Nonetheless, Latinos are not occupying positions of leadership in the country[54.] or in other sectors of the nation in relation to their numbers. No doubt it is partly because of a lack of clear government initiatives to include more of the Hispanic population. Yet on the other hand, could it also be that Hispanics are not adequately preparing and positioning themselves to assume greater responsibilities in the affairs of our nation? Are we preparing the next leaders, our children, so they will take on positions of greater responsibility? How may we positively influence the members of tomorrow's society? What will we do with this coming opportunity? For starters, let us become informed concerning important topics, let us know our representatives and leaders and let us exercise our right to vote. Those who cannot vote, motivate your children to vote and together let us assume greater political and social responsibility in the United States of America, where we live. Using our intelligence, vision and incentive, it is time to change our image and shine. Join together as Hispanic Americans with all of us who desire to make key contributions today! I believe in our culture and I believe it is time to wake up to take on the challenge in the era which we have been designated to live.

FOOTNOTES

[1] 1 John 3:29

[2] Revelation 5: 8-10

[3] Revelation 7:9

[4] Matthew 20:16

[5] Revelation 22:17

[6] Revelation 19:9

[7] John 14:2

[8] John 16:16-22

[9] Luke 10:11; Revelation 19:7

[10] Revelation 19:8

[11] Song of Solomon 4:10, 11

[12] Revelation 7:14

[13] Revelation 21:23

[14] Revelation17:14

[15] Revelation19:16

[16] Revelation 5:12

[17] I Corinthians 2:9

[18] Isaiah 62:2-5

[19] Revelation 7:17; 21:4

[20] Luke 9:2, 11, 10:9

[21] Isaiah 65:25

[22] Revelation 22:3

[23] Isaiah 9:7; Romans 14:17

[24] Luke 13:29

[25] Luke 14:15

[26] II Thessalonians 1:1-6

[27] Luke 13:28; Matthew 22:13, 25:30

[28] Revelation 19:9

[29] Matthew 22:4

[30] Mark 1:1

[31] John 3:15

[32] Mark 10:23

[33] John 3:3

[34] Mark 10:23; Mark 10:25

[35] Luke 6:20

[36] John 1:29

[37] I Peter 1:19-20

[38] I Peter 1:21

[39] John 14:6

[40] Matthew 25:31-46

[41] Luke 17:20-21

[42] Revelation 21:9

[43] Ephesians 5:25-27

[44] Luke 16:16-17

[45] Revelation 22:17

[46] Mark Hugo Lopez, and D'Vera Cohn, Hispanic Poverty Rate Highest In New Supplemental Census Measure, http://www.pewhispanic.org/2011/11/08/hispanic-poverty-rate-highest-in-new-supplemental-census-measure/ (November 2011).

[47] Between Two Worlds: How Young Latinos Come of Age in America, http://www.pewhispanic.org/2009/12/11/between-two-worlds-how-young-latinos-come-of-age-in-america/ (December 2009).

[48] U.S. Hispanic Country of Origin Counts for Nation Top 30 Metropolitan Areas, http://www.pewhispanic.org/2011/05/26/us-hispanic-country-of-origin-counts-for-nation-top-30-metropolitan-areas/ (May 2011).

[49] The Mexican-American Boom: Births Overtake Immigration, http://www.pewhispanic.org/2011/07/14/the-mexican-american-boom-brbirths-overtake-immigration/ (July 2011).

[50] The Dark Side of Illegal Immigration, http://www.usillegalaliens.com/impacts_of_illegal_immigration_crime.html

[51] Illegal Immigration: The $113 Billion Dollar Drain on the American Taxpayer, http://www.illegalimmigrationstatistics.org/illegal-immigration-a-113-billion-a-year-drain-on-u-s-taxpayers/#more-331(September 2011).

[52] We express our gratitude to Numbers USA, and the Center for Immigration Studies, for its valuable information concerning historic immigration data which we extracted from its web site.

[53] John Bersente, and Mark Howard, Why the Federal Government Can't Recruit and Retain Hispanic-Americans, http://www.ere.net/2010/01/27/why-the-federal-government-can%E2%80%99t-recruit-and-retain-hispanic-americans/ (January 2011).

[54] John Patrick and Donald Ritchie, The Oxford Guide to the United States Government (USA, Oxford University Press), (2001).

Israel, Dioselina, Elia, Gabriel, Mrs. Audelia Corona. Maria G. Erazo, Elena and Alma. (Left to right back row, then front row)

*Observations concerning my
areas I want to change*

_____

_____

_____

_____

_____

_____

_____

_____

_____

_____

_____

_____

_____

_____

_____

_____